TALES FROM A
SPORTING LIFE

TALES FROM A SPORTING LIFE

Percy Youd (1879-1963)

Memories of a Mersey man who made his mark

ISBN
1 901253 31 7
First published May 2003

Published by:
Léonie Press
an imprint of
Anne Loader Publications
13 Vale Road, Hartford,
Northwich, Cheshire CW8 1PL
Gt Britain
Tel: 01606 75660   Fax: 01606 77609
e-mail: anne@aloaderpubs.u-net.com
Website: www.anneloaderpublications.co.uk
www.leoniepress.com

Printed by:
Anne Loader Publications
Cover Lamination: The Finishing Touch, St Helens
Collation and Binding: B & S Swindells Ltd, Knutsford

Publisher's thanks

We are indebted to Mike Eddison, Local
Studies Advisor, Cheshire Record Office;
Rosemary Tyler, Curator of Local History,
Prescot Museum, Knowsley Museum Service;
Frodsham & District Local History Group;
the staff at Ellesmere Port Reference Library;
folk expert Roy Clinging; Alan Dickinson and
the Manchester Ship Canal Company;
Tom Hughes, Herbert Fletcher and other
kind collaborators for their valued help and
for permission to use many of the old
photographs reproduced in this book.
Thanks also to the Ordnance Survey for
extracts from their old maps.

Contents

List of illustrations

● *Percy Youd pictured in around 1918 (aged 38), in a formal portrait taken by national photographic chain Gales Studios Ltd and published as a postcard. It was posted (but an indistinct postmark omits to say where from) to his brother Horace c/o 12 Irwell Lane, Runcorn on March 1, 1918 and on the reverse Percy invites Horace "to come to see Liverpool, then to Whist Drive".*

INTRODUCING PERCY YOUD

Percy Youd was a "man's man". Born in 1879, in a Frodsham soon to be affected by the construction of the Manchester Ship Canal, he was a naughty wilful child who would probably have come to the attention of the juvenile courts had he lived 100 years later. He spent much of his boyhood "wagging" off school, which hampered his literacy, although his innate intelligence served him well at the time and for the rest of his life. He became a respected factory foreman, publican, First World War NCO and auctioneer – who knows what he might have done with a better education?

As a young man, he loved sport, fist-fighting and practical jokes, though he rarely drank – as a reaction against his father's frequent binges on the beer. He had one over-riding talent: he was a naturally gifted marksman, whether with a catapult, a muzzle-loader or a 12-bore shotgun. He was in his element wildfowling on the Mersey estuary and shooting in the nearby Cheshire hills. It wasn't long before local gambling men started to wager money on his results.

Percy was a good runner and his winning time in the gruelling Helsby Hill Race stood as a record for many years.

As a teenager he enjoyed playing the part of the Old Woman in the traditional "Soul-caking" play which he could remember by heart 60 years later.

At 13 he got a job for 5s 3d a week at the Telegraph Manufacturing Co. Ltd cable works in Helsby. In 1900, when he was 21, he tried his luck at the new smelting works in Ellesmere Port and in 1902 he was approached by his old firm when it merged with the British Insulated Wire Co. and asked

● *Percy in around 1927 (aged 48), when this card was posted to his sister Mrs Reed in Robin Hood Lane, Helsby on December 6. He writes that he "is sorry to say" their mother "is not very grand".*

to go the company's Prescot cable works as a foreman. In 1907 the management asked him to become tenant of the Greenall brewery's Imperial Hotel opposite the general office, which he soon built up into a significant sporting venue. His marksman's eye enabled him to have success in both bowls and billiards and he was enormously proud of his prowess in these sports. He did well when he competed in the local Walking Races, and also enjoyed football and rugby.

At the beginning of the First World War he joined the Army and his wife Sarah Jane (Sally) ran the Imperial in his absence. His family think that in 1918 she was so busy that she forgot to renew the licence. When he was demobbed the couple split up under the stress of this blow to Percy's lifestyle and it is significant that Sally is never mentioned by name in his writing. He refers to her only once, when telling the sad story of the death of three of their sons between 1909 and 1915. It does not occur to him to mention how they met (though she was a Helsby girl) or when they got married but it must have been in the early 1900s.

He then went to live in Rock Ferry and later Birkenhead. He set up as an auctioneer in a wooden building next to the Conservative Club in Westminster Road, Ellesmere Port, which had become a major political and social influence in his life. When he was much older, he moved to live in Ellesmere Port.

The common strand through all Percy's writing is his "macho" attitude to life and to physical pain. He recounts a terrifying accidental shooting, and stomach-turning medical procedures, which he bears stoically. It is impossible for the reader to tell if these stories are highly exaggerated or not. He also states that he suffered from recurring nightmares, so vivid

● *An undated photograph of Percy posing proudly with one of his many bowls trophies.*

that they made him scream aloud.

Percy was very much the centre of his own small male world and he was an inveterate name-dropper. He claims friendship with Selwyn Lloyd, the Conservative MP for Wirral who was Foreign Secretary at the time of the Suez Crisis and later Chancellor of the Exchequer, Lord Privy Seal, Leader of the House and Speaker of the Commons. Percy's family believe that Mr Lloyd attended his funeral, although we have been unable to confirm this as there is rather surprisingly no report of the event in the local paper. The famous politician, who lived at West Kirby, certainly visited Percy in hospital just before he died.

Percy will also always be remembered for his friendship with the Chinese dock labour leader Lock Ah Tam, who was convicted of murder under controversial circumstances. In 1926 Percy organised a 100,000-signature petition in a sadly fruitless attempt to save his friend from hanging.

His cavalier attittude to medicine and physical pain is thought to have contributed to his death. It is believed that at the age of 84, Percy was troubled by toothache and pulled out the offending tooth himself with a pair of rusty pliers. The socket became infected and he was taken fatally ill. He died at Clatterbridge Hospital, Bebington and is described on the death certificate as "a retired watchman".

went into IT the marsh ditches what we called bossing we used to thread bunch of worms on worsted about 7 yards long then wrap them around our fingers then slip them off in a bunch and tie them tightly with string then use stiff rod about 6 ft long and the string was about 6 ft then go in the main ditches You did not wait long for a bite and sometimes as many as 6 at a time would cling to the worms until you shook them off I have known them bite so quick I have had 3 men busy putting them in buckets they would bite so keen I thought their teeth must get stuck in the worsted it is great sport Bobbing for Eels I sometimes would have an Umbrella opened and pegged upside down tied to stake to throw them in until I had got as many as I wanted a large umbrella was very handy if you were where the grass was long or if it was going dark they seemed to bite better in the dark You never used a float you always feel them tugging at the worms there was about 9 boys in our gang one name Joey Ainsworth was almost twice as big as any others joined the Volunteers when 15 told them he was 18 only had not an helmet to fit him the head such a large head they had to MEASURE him for an helmet we were having a Hot Pot supper at the Town Hall one Saturday night I sat next to Joey who had 8 plate soup plates of hot pot I said everybody finished but you but he did not mind he said it was very good we went over to the commercial HOTEL after to have 2 Lemon Dashes he said I wont be long and went to the Back after about 10 minutes I went out and saw Him vomiting over a large Bowl He said I am coming now then taking a Red and

● A page from Percy Youd's story, written in biro on lined paper in a hard-back exercise book. The tale has no paragraphs – and no punctuation at all!

PUBLISHER'S NOTE

We make no apologies for the rather unusual format of this book, which has become more and more like a detective story since we first became associated with it. We hope you, too, enjoy piecing together all the clues.

In early 2002 Ken Bazley contacted us to ask if we would be interested in publishing the memoirs of his grandfather, George Thomas Percy Youd, which had been discovered posthumously. Ken had spent a great deal of time typing out the handwritten manuscript, which covered – in no particular order – various major events in the author's life. Ken felt strongly that the fragments should be preserved for posterity as evidence of a way of life that had gone for ever, especially as it contained the full script of the Frodsham version of the traditional Soul-caking play.

When we met, he showed us the original and the typescript that he had made from it. The text had been written on the lined pages of a blue hard-backed exercise book, in blue biro in the copperplate style taught to Victorian school children. The writing filled half the book, with random capital letters sprinkled throughout, no punctuation and no paragraphs – just a solid daunting "lump" of 22,000 words.

According to the notes on the inside front cover the account had been started on Monday, 17th December 1956, when Percy Youd was 77, and lived at Marsh Farm Cottage Pontoon, Ellesmere Port, beside the Ship Canal near the present Boat Museum. He had continued it after buying and moving to 1 Grace Road, Ellesmere Port on 11 November 1957. He wrote: "I have been asked to write a life story of my schooldays and

● *A Youd family portrait taken in the orangery at the Imperial Hotel, Prescot, before 1914. Back: Percy Snr; middle row: Sally with baby Leslie and daughter Winifred; front row: sons Percy Jnr and Gerald. Note the magnificent cat (right). Percy also had prizewinning Dalmatians and a menagerie of other creatures.*

At this time, Len and Cyril had died and Phyllis was not yet born. Sidney, who was severely handicapped, is not pictured. He died in 1915.

after", and had tried out two titles: "Percy Youds Schooldays" and "A Country Lads Naughty Tricks – All True Stories."

I skimmed through Ken's version and thought he had done a remarkable job of transcribing the text into conventional sentences and spellings. The book's contents intrigued me but as soon as I started to look at it in greater detail I realised that it would have to be sympatheically edited, too. Ken had been faithful to Percy's telegrammatic style, which added interest in small doses but was impossible to read at length. I decided that I should use my experience as an editor to "breathe on it" gently to help it flow without altering its character.

There was also the big question of continuity. It was not possible to divide the "lump" into chapters because after the initial pieces about his youth, Percy almost never mentioned dates and jumped about from one part of his life to another in his stream-of-consciousness story. I decided to break it all up into short sections separated by asterisks to give the eye and the brain some relief.

Ken and his wife Gaynor had done as much research as they could to collaborate Percy's account, but it would still have been very difficult to decide what went where if we had tried to present the reader with a chronological story. We therefore agreed to leave the tales in the order in which they had been written.

Percy's story is a tantalising fragment which tells carefully selected parts of his life, and asks almost more questions than it answers. In many places he assumes knowledge that a modern reader would not have.

I have therefore decided that rather than using lots of appendices at the end of the book to explain or illustrate the text,

● *Left: Phyllis Bazley (Percy's daughter) and right: Ken Bazley, his grandson*

● *The house in Grace Road, Ellesmere Port (as it is now), where Percy lived from 1957 until he died in September 1963. The Bazleys found the blue exercise book containing his manuscript on the floor here when they were clearing out the property. (Photograph taken by AL).*

Percy's story should be printed uninterrupted on the right-hand pages of the book, whilst reproducing on the left-hand pages, old photographs of where he lived and worked, old maps showing some of the places mentioned in the text, modern pictures showing some of these sites as they are now, and official documents relating to the deaths of himself, his wife and three of their children. We also include press cuttings about Lock Ah Tam and Selwyn Lloyd plus a lot of other background information that we have researched about places associated with him.

Part two of the book is an account by Percy's daughter Phyllis (Ken's mother) of her miserable childhood with him and the woman with whom he lodged. Immediately after her parents were estranged, she went to live with her mother in Helsby but was then abducted twice by Percy to his lodgings in Birkenhead. Having lost three children in infancy, he obviously missed the surviving youngsters and was happy to provide fatherly treats but couldn't substitute for their mother's care. He palmed Phyllis and her brother Leslie off on their eccentric landlady and although he loved his children and meant them no harm he was too wrapped up in himself to be aware of his daughter's suffering.

It is hard not to judge Percy by the standards of today, but his story needs to be read against the backdop of Victorian values and the pervading male-dominated ethos of the time.

We have been completely true to Percy's original and no significant changes have been made; I must claim responsibility for the explanatory text on the facing pages, which I hope readers will find illuminating.

Anne Loader, April 2003

● *Cliff View where Percy Youd was born in 1879. It was also known as "Booth Street" because many of the residents were called Booth. The houses must have been new then as they are not on the 1873-4 OS map. (Photo by AL).*

● *Moreton Terrace, opposite, where Percy used to hide in the unfinished buildings. (Pictured in 2002 by AL).*

GEORGE THOMAS PERCY YOUD

AN AUTOBIOGRAPHY

I was born at Booth Street, Marsh Green, Frodsham, Cheshire on 30th July, 1879. My father's name was Samuel Youd, and my mother's name was Eliza Spruce before marriage. Her father, George Spruce, was murdered at Chester when she was about 14 years of age. Tom Hart of Warrington was tried for the murder, but the verdict returned was 'not guilty'.

My grandfather, who kept a beer-house called the Cheshire Cheese with his wife Elizabeth, was named Thomas Youd and he held the licence before the Manchester Ship Canal was starting to be made. There was a great lot of navvies used to call at the Cheshire Cheese because it was the nearest pub to the canal about two miles away. It was a great sporting beer-house, there used to be rabbit coursing, pigeon shooting, domino matches, puff darts etc. and some great fights.

When I was only 11 years old I bought and trapped 148 pigeons one day for some great shooting men from many miles around.

About the time Moreton Terrace was being built I used to go to Overton School but not very often – I used to play truant ('wag') and sometimes stayed out all night, although my father offered me 6d for every full week I went to school. I only managed to do one full week. After playing truant over a week, I saw my mother going to the grocer's near our house, so I rushed in, got a slice of bread and butter then unhooked the

● *Overton Hill in the early 1900s.*
(Postcard from AL's collection).

● *Overton East in the early 1900s, pictured from the parish church tower. The school on the left replaced the one attended (occasionally!) by Percy Youd. It was opened in November 1892, the year that he left. At 8.57am each day the bell in the tower summoned the boys to roll-call. (Postcard from AL's collection).*

parlour window so I could sneak in later that night.

My dad used to go every night to the Cheshire Cheese which was only 130 yards from our house and he always stayed until closing time. When he arrived home my mother said: "Percy has not come home yet and it is a cold frosty night, he may be sleeping in the new houses."

Moreton Terrace was a row of about 14 houses which were yet without doors and windows, and Mother asked Dad to go with her and look in every room in each house. They each took a box of matches and a few candles and were searching until after midnight before going home to Booth Street only 50 yards away. They never thought I was in bed and being so tired did not think of looking in the children's room. As I had gone through the garden window, looking out of the parlour, I had taken my boots off before creeping up the stairs. They were between the kitchen and parlour doors which were often closed to keep the draught out. My mother had locked the doors. When I got up, she said she would see I did go to school that day so after breakfast she got hold of me to take me to Overton School about 1½ miles from our house. When we got to the top of Church Field by the Church we met old Mr. Nield the blacksmith, holding on to his two sons, Fred and Alf Nield, tied with a clothes line. They were my truant pals, so we were only few hundred yards from school when they made a dash for freedom still tied together. I also broke loose and dashed after them and when we got few a hundred yards away I untied them. We then made off towards Delamere Forest which was a favourite haunt of ours.

On the previous Monday we had spent a nice time in Delamere Forest. I had my school money with me, 3d, which

● *Modern exterior of the Iron Church (St Dunstan's) in Main Street, which was used to accommodate the parishioners of St Lawrence when the main church was being repaired and extended from 1880-1883. It could seat 230. It was moved forward some years ago to improve access to flats at the rear. (Photo by AL).*

● *Iron Church interior, around 1880s. (Photograph reproduced by kind permission of Frodsham & District Local History Group).*

we were supposed to pay weekly. We met a bread van and bought a 3d loaf. We had no pocket knife but broke it up best we could to share it and none was wasted; we enjoyed it and were well satisfied. We often fed off some farmer's swedes when we were playing truant.

✳

I lost one of my best school chums, a boy named Tom Raynor, who was drowned at the clay pits while bathing. I think it was about 1889. We were nearly always together but this night I had gone to get wimberries on Overton Hills and he would not come. He was swimming across what we called the 6ft. flash water singing "Life on the ocean wave," then must have had cramp, for he was dead when they got him out. The day they had the inquest I was playing truant and saw the jury coming past the Iron Church in Main Street where we used to attend some Sunday nights. We used to sit in the back seats opposite the man who tolled the bell and play a game of cards called "All Fours," a game of seven-up for ½d. a game, anyone getting four times (high, low, Jack, game) in one hand won. But one Sunday the bell ringer stopped me, saying: "You are the ring-leader and don't you come any more in this church."

I always carried a catapult and was a very good shot so I concealed myself in the shrubs and waited until he had stopped ringing the bell, then got my catapult out of my pocket. I had a pocketful of marbles then started to shoot at the bell and "dong, dong, dong," it rang out. The congregation kept looking around at the old bell man who could not understand why the bell kept on ringing. My pals said: "He must have

● *Main Street, Frodsham in the early 1900s, taken from the east. (Postcard from AL's collection).*

● *The Cheshire Cheese, Main Street, formerly a Greenalls alehouse run by Thomas and Elizabeth Youd, Percy's grandparents, between 1869-1898 and frequented by men building the Manchester Ship Canal. Next door, on the right, is West Bank where Thomas Bate the vet is recorded in Morris and Co's Directory as living in 1874. By 1882 Alexander Bate was listed in Kelly's Directory instead of him. The garden backs on to Marsh Lane. (Photo by AL).*

gone on the roof." I was concealed among the laurel trees until I had shot all my marbles at the old bell and I did not miss once. It was a nice clear moonlit night.

We used to be always doing things we should not do: we would sometimes turn the gas lamps out and dare each other to do wicked things such as opening the doors of houses and throwing old cans inside.

The row of cottages called Booth Street was about 21 houses with a dead end. On the right was a large timber yard and a stack yard at the bottom of Booth Street was boarded with a 9ft. fence. At the front of the houses was a garden just the width of each house and about 20 yards long. Small rails about 3ft. high divided each garden. Nearly all the houses used the garden to dry their washing and some people used to leave their clothes lines out after they took washing into their house. One night there were about five of us. I got our gang to cut a clothes line or two, and each of the gang was told to tie four houses' door knobs together. When all was tied, at a signal by lighting a match, each boy was told to knock hard with a stone then make a rush for a gap in the hedge half-way between the row of houses into Tom Ainsworth's farm stack yard, then go through his hedge-bottom stack yard, across a field below the houses then into Davies' stack yard and saw mill, then come into Marsh Lane and walk down as if we had been up the Main Street. When we met the crowd there were still some busy untying the clothes line that fastened their doors. I used to always be blamed as the ringleader but I asked how could it be us as we had been up Main Street. We had another trick of always turning the lamps out near Marsh Lane and often got chased by the police.

7

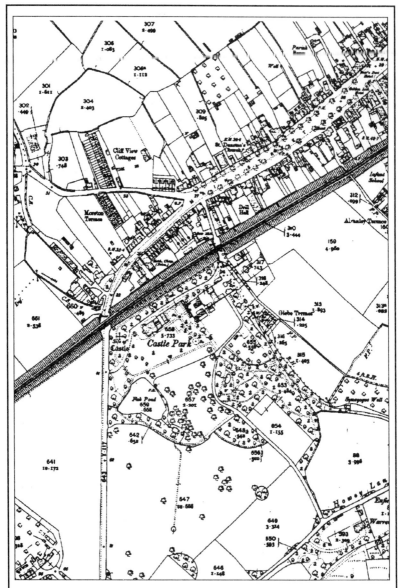

● *Map of Frodsham taken from the Third Edition 25-inch to the mile Ordnance Survey of Cheshire, which was first produced in 1870 and updated between 1904-10.*

When we were making more noise than usual playing 'Kick Bung' with an old salmon tin or a corned beef can at night, we knew the police would soon be after us. We also used to delight in playing 'Tick Tack' with a button and pin and reel of black thread. We would stick the pin in a window frame then slowly pull the thread and hear the button going 'tick-tack' before being found out or chased.

One night I did one of my jokes on an old shoemaker named Swift Peacock, whose wife used to drink a lot and get drunk. She would ask me to go to the Cheshire Cheese pub to fetch her a pint or a quart of beer, and I'd sometimes get a penny or a halfpenny. He used to keep a lot of hens, and eggs were then about 18 for a shilling. He had a medium-sized clothes basket nearly always half-full of eggs on a form opposite the back door, and a paraffin lamp burning. He used to do his shoemaking in the front room. He was a fat old man, and thrashed his wife Anne a lot for getting drunk – she used to scream murder. One night the gang dared me to throw half a brick into his basket of eggs and I did, I must have broken more than a dozen. It was a night he had been thrashing Anne and I was sorry for the old woman, who used to sometimes sell the eggs for beer money. One time when he had been thrashing her for drinking she picked the rolling pin up and smashed a lot of the eggs shouting "revenge is sweet!"

One night a boy named Fred Parker threw a small swede turnip through the window. I think now that we should have been caught for the wicked things we'd done.

There was a Veterinary Surgeon Farrier named Alec Bate who lived in a large house in Main Street and whose garden came down to nearly opposite Booth Street. He was often seen

PIGEON SHOOTING AND CLAY PIGEON SHOOTING c1911

Pigeon shooting is a form of sport consisting of shooting at live pigeons released from traps. The number of traps, which are six-sided boxes falling flat open at the release of a spring, is usually five; these are arranged 5 yds apart on the arc of a circle of which the shooter forms the centre. The distance (maximum) is 31 yds, handicapping being determined by shortening the distance.

The five traps are each connected by wires with a case ("the puller"); a single string pulled by a man stationed at the side of the shooter works an arrangement of springs and cog-wheels in the "puller," and lets fall one of the traps; it is impossible to know beforehand which trap will be re]eased.

At a fixed distance from the centre of the traps is a boundary within which the birds hit must fall if they are to count to the shooter. This line varies in distance in the various clubs; the National Gun Club boundary being 65 yds, that of the Monaco Club being only 20 yds.

The charge of shot allowed must not exceed 1¼ oz. The best type of pigeon is the blue rock.

From the start of the Hurlingham Club at Fulham in 1867 pigeon-shooting was a favourite sport there; it was, however, stopped in 1906.

The principal pigeon shooting centre in England is now at the National Gun Club grounds at Hendon. The great international competitions and sweepstakes take place at Monaco (see page 117).

An artificial bird of clay, now more usually of a composition of pitch, is often substituted for the live pigeon. These clay birds are also sprung from traps. This sport originated in the United States, where, under the name of "trap-shooting," or inanimate bird shooting, it is extremely popular.

At first the traps invented threw the birds with too great a regularity of curve; now the traps throw the birds at different and unknown angles, and the skill required is great.

In clay-bird shooting the traps usually number fifteen, and are out of sight of the shooter. The Inanimate Bird Shooting Association in England was started in 1893.

(From 1911 Encyclopaedia accessed on Internet; no name)

going in his pony and trap towards Sutton Weaver and when his apples were ripe if we saw him going out we would rob his orchard. I would throw my cap over the hedge after we had thrown lots of stones knocking the apples off, then go to Mrs. Bate and say: "My mother has asked me to come to ask you, will you please let me get my cap – a boy has thrown it over the hedge into your garden."

She'd say: "Go and get it yourself."

I would then collect the apples and pass them through the hedge to the gang.

✳

I was a terror for fighting even before I left school and, as I said, was a grand shot with a catapult. My cousin Albert Youd would hold a match up for me to shoot at and strike it. I shot many stray pigeons with my catapult. We used to go tracing wild birds one or two each side of a hedge. In the marshes we killed many blackbirds and thrushes, even Jenny Wrens – the marshes were a great place for wild birds. Many wild ducks and wild geese would be shot when it was a hard winter.

There were several using the old muzzle guns in them days. One of the greatest shots was a man named Postman Parker who was once matched to shoot against a man for £5 and a pig. He had a man who used to load his gun out of the powder and shot bags. Before the date of the match someone brought this man over to throw Parker over. After killing four birds each, Parker's opponent missed his fifth bird; then the loader only put powder in Parker's gun but pretended to put shot in. When the trap was pulled the pigeon flew straight towards Parker who shot when the bird was not many yards from him.

SYNAGOGUE WELL

● *Synagogue Well, pictured c1900 as Percy Youd would have known it. (Photograph reproduced by kind permission of Frodsham & District Local History Group).*

The well is situated down a path in Castle Park and was capped over with concrete in the 1920s after several drownings and at least one suicide.

It was once the main source of water for people in the town centre. The overflow came down Fountain Lane and joined the stream which ran along Main Street.

The well became dry when Warrington Corporation bored for water at Fox Hill in the 1930s.

Its history is unknown and the origin of its name is uncertain, though it is said to have been walled in medieval times by an itinerant Jew in gratitude for its cooling water.

A hardy 19th century curate, the Rev Shadwell, is reported to have taken a dip in the well every morning even when it was frozen over and he had to break the ice.

The wad must have struck the pigeon on the head for Parker picked it up still only stunned. It came out months later about this curious thing, but Parker won the money and pig.

We used to have great fun with the old muzzle-loading guns by shooting at swinging lighted candles hung from the ceiling by 6ft wire. The draught from the fired cap would blow the candle out if you were on the target, and you had to fire before the third swing. I won many coppers at this game before I left school.

＊

One of my favourite spots where I spent many hours was Synagogues [sic] Well where many suicides have taken place. It was natural springs, very clear and about 10ft deep, 12ft long and about 12ft wide. If you threw a marble or a coin in, it had many colours when lying on the bottom – yellow, blue, green and red, like a rainbow – and the water was icy cold. It must have been many hundred years old.

There was a 9ft high fence about 5ft away which belonged to Castle Park. We used to often go into the park woods when playing truant, but only at noon when the gardeners had gone for dinner. My uncle Jack Youd was Head Gardener, he was the eldest son of my granddad who was licensee of the Cheshire Cheese in them days.

There was an article in the *Chester Chronicle* two or three years ago [about 1954-55; Ed] about Castle Park written by a man named Hutton under the title of 'Main Street', to say it never was a castle but a large mansion burnt down many years ago. I wish to contradict his report for I read a book published

● *The Misses Wright with Mr Bean the coachman, in front of their red sandstone mansion, c1900. (Photograph reproduced by kind permission of Frodsham & District Local History Group).*

● *Castle Park lake, c1899 – illicit haunt of little boys with fishing rods! Like Synagogue Well, it dried up after Warrington Corporation bored for water at Fox Hill in the 1930s. (Photograph reproduced by kind permission of Frodsham & District Local History Group).*

in 1806 called the "Gazetteer of England and Wales". There was six volumes so I thought I would look at what it said about my birthplace Frodsham. It said: "Small town a mile or two from the River Mersey where there was a castle many years ago where lived the last reigning Prince of Wales whose name was Llewellin who marched his men from there to Chester and beheaded the Governor of Chester Castle, then marched to Hawarden Castle and beheaded the Governor of Hawarden Castle, was later captured and the first man recorded to be Hung, Drawn, and Quartered in England, and his quarters were burnt at the stake in different parts of England." I think the date given was about 1050, the castle was burnt down later and a mansion built.

It was at a later time owned by an old gentleman named Edward Abbott Wright who bought it in 1861 and died in 1891. I think he had two daughters who were not married and they lived there many years. After their father died they often used to drive out in an open carriage and pair when it was fine. They had beautiful horses and their coachman, Mr. Bean, was always very smart and wore livery. The Misses Wright were very sedate and let the public into their garden and park every Whit Monday.

Every Christmas they would get their gardeners (about four men) to cut holly and shrubs to give to the public for Christmas decorations. There was a large lake between the gardens and the park. There was a lovely show of flowers to be seen at Whitsuntide, with many colours of azaleas, rhododendrons, roses and lots of other nice flowers. I have often gone to steal a bamboo cane – they used to grow in shallow water between the lake and park wood, about ½ mile from the foot of Overton

● *Castle Park gardener in 1899. Kelly's Directory of 1914 says the grounds covered 30 acres. (Photograph reproduced by kind permission of Frodsham & District Local History Group).*

● *Caves near Overton Hill pictured in the early 1900s. (Postcard from AL's collection).*

Hills. They were 6ft. and over, and we used them as fishing rods and to get some of the fish from the lake when gardeners had gone for dinner.

＊

An old hermit used to live about the hills and sleep in the caves about a mile away. His name was Old George Thompson. He wore a long shabby grey coat which came down nearly to his boots, and many children were frightened of him, but I was very friendly with him and have many times given him my 3d school money when I met him. He would tell me he had not had anything to eat for two days. He would sketch me drawings of old Overton Church, for he always had a box of coloured crayons and an old pocket book. He was then about 70 years old, and he said he would eat young grass or dandelions when he was very hungry. He would come into Frodsham then go back to the hills; sometimes people would give him coppers and something to eat. He used to have an old red and white handkerchief to tie his bundle of food. If anyone gave him coppers he would sometimes buy a loaf of bread.

If I told my mother I had given Old George Thompson my school money because he'd had nothing eat for two days she would not thrash me. She was very good to the poor and in them days used to go out washing for 1/6d a day, four or five days a week, because my father went on the booze for a week or two and we would not have food for days. He did love beer.

＊

SOULCAKING

● *Soulcaking runs in both sides of Ken Bazley's family. His grandfather Percy took part in the 1890s, and his father Edwin Bazley of Helsby is shown second left, in the pointed hat, in this old photograph from around 1925, entitled "Soul-cakers, Helsby". (Photo courtesy of Jones's Ale Soulcakers).*

Soulcaking is a Cheshire custom that is still being kept alive by a small number of local groups, but was once much more widespread.

It is a subject on which there are many hotly-contested schools of thought, and the editor is indebted to the sources mentioned in the bibliography, but the following is a basic layman's guide:

Those taking part would go from house to house, singing either a begging song or a plea for prayers for the dead. They would put on a mummer's play and then receive special cakes, money or a drink as a reward. Nowadays, most soulcaking takes place in public houses!

Performances were held around Hallowe'en, (October 31), All Souls Eve/All Saints Day (November 1) and (All Souls Day) November 2, depending upon the community tradition. The dates coincided with the beginning of winter and the widespread belief that at this time of year spirits walked abroad and ancestors should be worshipped.

Soulcakes were originally food left out to appease the

continued p20

18

We had an old yearly custom called Soulcaking. A gang composed of eight or nine would go to houses singing:

Here's one or two or three good hearty lads
and we are all in one mind,
this night we are coming souling
and we hope you'll prove kind
with your ale and good beer,
and we'll come no more souling till this time next year.

God bless the master of this house and the mistress also
likewise the little children around your table door
and if you will give us just one drink of your good beer
we will come no more souling till this time next year.

Now open the doors to let our merry actors in,
we hope to fight and win,
whether we rise or stand or fall.

We do our best to please you all,
if you don't believe in what I say
step in King George so clear the way.
In comes I, King George, to fight the Valiant Soldier,
if you don't believe in what I say
step in the Valiant Soldier so clear the way.

In comes I, the valiant soldier, to fight King George,
Slasher is my name England is my Nation,
Frodsham is my dwelling place,
and God is my Salvation.

SOULCAKING continued

dead spirits. They were small and round, made of light dough, well spiced and sweetened.

Though the words for each area's play are slightly different, they all have a theme of a challenge, a battle, a death and a magical revival, and a cast of players which includes a symbolic horse called "Dick" or "Dicky Dalton". This appears in an interlude operated by a man draped in a sheet carrying a mask made from a horse's skull, whose hinged lower jaw could be made to snap or bite.

The other characters and the main plot are very close to mumming, with King George, an opponent whom he slays, the Devil, the old woman and a quack doctor.

Soulcaking is thought to date back to around the tenth century but its origins seem to be pagan. The horse's presence, also known as "hodening" and present in other folk customs, may be linked to the Norse god Odin.

However, in the more recent past it was just a good time-honoured way – for villagers like young Percy Youd in the 1890s – to have some fun and free drinks in the company of friends (and maybe an excuse to visit some of the posher houses in the district).

Because, for generations, the people who performed the soulcaking plays could not read or write, the tradition is oral and there are fascinating difference between the various 'scripts' and even in the actual names given to the characters.

For instance, Beelzebub (The Devil) is 'Belshie Bob' in Percy's version of the Frodsham play, and 'Belzebub' in nearby Halton. There are also differences between Percy's version and a later one recalled by Bob Baxter of Frodsham: though they obviously come from the same root.

Percy doesn't write the play out like a script with each character's name in the margin, but merely mentions them in passing, since he obviously knows everyone's part by heart. They would appear to be the "Letter-in" who asks for the doors to be opened, King George, the Valiant Soldier (in some plays he is 'Colonel Slasher'), the Old Woman, the Doctor, Belshie Bob, Old Derry Doubt, Little Box, Dick the Horse's Head and the un-named man who leads him (called the Driver in some other plays).

Sometimes it seems that various traditions have got

continued p22

King George, what are thou but a silly boy,
I've come to fight thee King George.

Get away thou silly lad, I cut thee
and make thy body full of holes
before thou art three days older.

How canst thou make my body full of holes
when my head is made of iron,
my body made of steel,
my hands and feet are knuckle bone,
I challenge thee on the field. Prepare!

Then three clashes with swords then the Valiant Soldier falls
wounded. The Old Woman comes rushing in, shouting:
Oh King George what hast thou done,
gone and killed my only son and heir,
see how he now lies bleeding there.

The old woman then cries:
£5 for a doctor £10 if he is a good one.

In comes I, the doctor, bold and brave
to try to cure the soldier King George has slain.

Old woman cries:
How comest thou to be a doctor?

who cries:
By my travels, I've travelled high,

SOULCAKING continued

muddled up. Robert Holland wrote, in 1886, more or less contemporaneously with Percy's experiences: "As far as I can ascertain, several customs which were formerly distinct and which took place at different times of the year, are now confounded together, and all take place at the same time of year. These customs were Soulcaking proper, which took place on All Souls' Eve; the performance of a mock-heroic play, which, I suspect, was originally performed at Easter, but which in many counties is now acted at Christmas; and the 'Dobby Horse' performance, which I think may have been part of the Christmas mummings.

"Nowadays, the 'acting' as it is called is combined with this; but the actors still begin their operations by singing a Souling song outside the door. Having finished the song, the 'actors' knock at the door and beg to be admitted. to the kitchen. Leave is generally granted and all the family and servants assemble to see the performance.

"The words are entirely traditional, being handed down orally from one generation to another; consequently many palpable errors have crept in

● *Ken Bazley, who was a soulcaker for 20 years, pictured in 1985 as Colonel Slasher (a part also known as the Valiant Soldier).*

and the text varies in almost every village."

There's a lovely quote from *The Cheshire Sheaf* in 1880, which reports that: "Three middle-aged men, with a concertina, have just been Souling here. They began well but ended with very bad verses about ale and strong beer which, they said, was all for which they came."

Perhaps the spirit of Soulcaking can be summed up in these words attributed to the modern Comberbach Soulcakers, whose motto is said to be: "Never knowingly under-rehearsed...!"

I've travelled low,
where the wind never blew
and the cock never crew,
here Jack take three sniffs out of this bottle
if thou not be quite dead rise up and fight thy battle.

Valiant Soldier rises, saying:
Oh my back, terrible aches and pains,
if you don't believe in what I say
enter Old Belshie Bob so clear the way.

In comes I, Old Belshie Bob,
on my shoulder I carry a pail
in my hand a dripping pan
I think myself a jolly old man,
if you don't believe in what I say,
enter Old Derry Doubt and clear the way.

In comes I, Old Derry Doubt, with my shirt lap out,
four yards in and five yards out,
if you don't believe in what I say
enter in Little Box so clear the way.

In comes I, Little Box,
under my arm I carry a box,
this box is made of the very best wood
a few coppers will do it no harm,
a few shillings will do it some good,
if you don't believe in what I say
enter in the Horse's Head so clear the way.

● *Huts in one of the settlements on the banks of the Manchester Ship Canal built by the enlightened contractor Thomas Walker to house the navvies and their families. They were well built and had good sanitary arrangements. He also provided schools, hospitals and missionaries to cater for their educational, health and spiritual needs. (Photo reproduced by kind permission of the Manchester Ship Canal Company).*

● *Navvies at work. (Photo courtesy of Cheshire Record Office)*

Then comes the horse, with a man under a horse-cloth with a wooden prop under the horse's head, led by a man who cries:

In comes Dick with all his men,
he has come to see you once again,
once he was alive but now he is dead.
He has travelled high and been on show
and would go anywhere he had to.
Now Ladies and Gentlemen please open your heart
and spare few coppers to buy Dick a new cart.

Sometimes we would get a few coppers and sometimes cake or a drink. I used to take the Old Woman's part.

I left Frodsham when I was about 16 years old to go to Helsby.

✳

There were plenty of ells ('snigs' we called them) in the ditches on the marshes, there must have been millions. In the winter they would go in the crevices between the stones at the bottom of the walls of the road bridges. These were on the roads leading to the huts on the banks where the Manchester Ship Canal ran, which were built to house the many navvies and their wives and children. The main ditches were about two miles long on either side of the road. All other ditches in the marshes used to run into these before going into the Mersey later. The bridges over the main ditches were about 9 or 10 feet wide over the top going into the field but only about 3ft. wide below for the water to run under and about 4ft. high. We used to make dams of mud and clay about a yard from each end then bail the water out with buckets until it was dry, then the

● *Scenes from Ince Marshes: reed-lined road and a network of drainage ditches crossed by bridges. (Photos by AL).*

ells would come wriggling out of the walls before we put them in buckets. It was best to do this in winter and we could always find a ready market for them.

✳

There were many well-known characters in Frodsham: one well-known family of bricksetters, Dan, Fred and George Garner, were good workmen who all liked beer. Dan, who committed suicide, drowned himself in Synagogues Well saying on the note he left: "God says there is forgiveness at the 11th hour and it is now just 11 o'clock."

Another well-known character was Old Father Brown who the Vicar Mr. Henry Blogg of Overton Vicarage met one day and said, "Drunk again!"

Brown replied: "So am I."

He used to sleep in Alec Bate's stable and was found dead there many years ago. There was a good yarn about him: a school pal who had been to America 40 years before came over on a holiday and was asking in the Bear's Paw Hotel if Old Father Brown was still alive. Someone said: "Yes, he is one amongst that crowd at the corner of Church Street."

The friend said: "Fetch him in," and when he came said: "I guess you will have a pint."

Father Brown said: "Yes, thank you."

Shortly afterwards the friend said: "I guess you will have another pint?"

Father Brown replied: "Yes and thy are a good guesser."

Father soon drank that pint, then the man said: "Guess you will have another?"

Father said: "Thy are the best guesser I ever met."

HELSBY CABLE WORKS

● *Senior management at Helsby cable works, c1900. In the front row from the left are E Crosland (general manager), James Taylor (director) and George Crosland Taylor (director-engineer). (Photograph reproduced by kind permission of Frodsham & District Local History Group).*

George Crosland Taylor was sent by his industrialist father to the International Electrical Exhibition in Paris in 1881 and immediately foresaw electricity's potential for telecommunications.

In 1882 he set up an engineering firm in Neston and started to make telegraph apparatus and accessories. Then during a visit to London he came across a new process for insulating wires with gutta percha which he thought was very promising. After a false start he developed a machine to do the job, which required a 300ft-long shed and 300 gallons of cooling water an hour. He persuaded his brother James Taylor and James' brother-in-law Fred Whitley to put up the extra capital he needed to develop and exploit the process.

In 1886 the three men agreed to join forces with their agent James Slater-Lewis of Helsby, who had invented a screw-top porcelain insulator and manufactured batteries in a shed at the rear of his house. He joined the board as managing director.

The site at Neston had soon proved unsuitable and the company decided to move to Helsby. The village was ideal for their purposes as it had two railways, an abundant natural water supply

continued p30

28

The friend kept guessing until Father Brown got drunk.

✳

I left school when I was 13 years old and had only just passed into 4th Standard. I went to Helsby Cable Works, then owned by the late James Taylor and his brother Crosland Taylor, and got a job at 5s 3d week. I had to be there at 6.30am – there were no buses then. We had to walk 2½ mile; we had a break of half an hour at 8.30am then worked from 9am till 12 noon, then 1pm till 6 o'clock. I was there three year before I lost half an hour. I was on night duty when I was only 14 year old – they did not mind then, over 60 years ago. I think the Helsby Works was the first to come on the 48-hour week. We used to sometimes not go to bed till the afternoon.

One morning, me and Sam Antrobus were sitting on the old Brook ('Bruck' we called it) Stone, a large granite 'resting' stone about ½ ton which has been lying over for 100 years on the junction at the bottom of Main Street and Marsh Lane. We were just talking about our night work at Helsby Works when Sam said: "Look at the great lot of balloons on yonder rag cart, all colours. I bet thee thou cannot burst half a dozen for a packet of Woodbines or a packet of Cinderallas."

I said: "It's on."

Guessing that he was going down to Booth Street, the man was only walking beside his cart more than 100 yards away. I ran down Marsh Lane towards Booth Street through Davies' big stack yard gate where they stored drain pipes, chimley pots, bricks etc.. The hedge was about 6ft high. I waited a short while until the rag cart was level with me, then threw some

HELSBY CABLE WORKS continued

at a constant temperature of 54°F via a borehole, and space for expansion.

The firm, now called the Telegraph Manufacturing Company, bought land close to the Cheshire Lines Railway. The clay bricks to construct what became the Britannia Works were made on the spot from the sub-soil and the hole left from the excavations was later used as a condensing pool for the boilers. It held 500,000 gallons of water.

Prouction started in 1887. Over the next few years the new works prospered and expanded, taking on some troublesome pioneering jobs which taxed the workers' ingenuity.

By 1895 the Helsby works employed 350 people – including Percy and many of his friends. The products they made included vulcanised rubber insulated wires and cables, other wires with various coverings and telephone switchboards.

The company continued to grow and – needing more capital – in 1902 amalgamated with the British Insulated Wire Company of Prescot. The new firm called itself the British Insulated and Helsby Cables Ltd.

It was just after this merger that Percy was approached to go

● *Helsby cable works at lunchtime early in 1910. It would have changed little since Percy's days there as a youth in the 1890s – apart from an abortive attempt to manufacture car tyres from 1905-1912. Another diversification, in 1898, was into golf ball production using the employees' skills in handling gutta percha. (Photo reproduced by kind permission of the Frodsham & District Local History Group).*

large clinkers right amongst the balloons. There was a large number busted, then I ran through the stack yard and came through a couple of fields that brought me to behind the Iron Church which is about 100 yards from the Bruck Stone where Sammy was still laughing. I was very sorry after and told him it was his fault and we ought to be locked up. He gave me the penny for cigarettes.

He was always prompting me to do some trick. We used to wrap some old sacks tied with string in the shape of football to pretend we were shooting goals at supper time. So one night I got a large iron ball nearly as big as a football and wrapped an old sack around it. When a man named Arnold Turner came in, I shouted "Shoot, Arnold!" and pretended to be a goalkeeper. He took a running kick then howled with pain. They had to take him home, and he was off work many weeks. I nearly got the sack over this soft joke.

One night after midnight I was very sleepy so one of the chaps said: "Go and have an hour in that empty cotton skip."

It was about 6ft by 4ft and had a swinging lid. I had not been in long when the old watchman Josh Atherton lifted the lid and asked: "What are you doing there?"

I replied: "Looking for a mouse."

He often said to me after: "Have you caught that mouse yet?"

One night the foreman was a decent chap named Earnshaw who was courting a niece from the Robin Hood Hotel in Helsby. Some nights he used to lean on the big iron pillars near the braiding machines and often fell asleep. Me and Sammy were on a cotton winding machine about 20 yards from where Mr. Earnshaw was snoozing. Sammy said: "When he nods off,

● *When this 1930 aerial shot was taken the BICC site had grown enormously. This extract from a larger picture shows where the original Britannia Telegraph Works of the British Insulated and Helsby Cables Ltd. was situated. (Photo reproduced by kind permission of Frodsham & District Local History Group).*

● *The 'Bruck Stone' in 2002. (Photo by AL).*

Percy, could you hit him on the head with bale of cotton?" They were about half the size of a rugby football.

I said: "I'll try," and very soon I did. He had only nodded off a few minutes when I threw a bale and it hit him right on the jaw. He clung to the iron pillar dazed, looked at the chaps working the braiding machines before he could get his speech and then shouted: "Who done that?"

They were all still laughing when he came to the winding machines and said: "Did you see that, Percy?"

I looked amazed and asked: "See what?"

He said: "Someone threw a bale of cotton at me when I was nodding!"

I said: "Who was you nodding to?"

He never found out. He was very careful after that.

*

There was a farm garden fence came near to Bruck Stone, and a man named Andrews was the farmer. He had one daughter, Emily, and one son called Jimmy who kept a few pigeons. My cousin William Henry Youd was a partner with Jimmy Andrews. A hundred yards away Alec Bate the Vet kept many pigeons and one of Jimmy Andrew's pigeons went and stayed with Alec Bate's flock. When Jimmy went to ask for it back he chased him with a whip. Jimmy was upset because it was his favourite Black Hen, so they asked me if I would try and get it.

I said: "If he goes out in the trap, I'll go up loft and try and get the Black Hen."

The loft was over a loose box and there was several puppies

● *Above and below: some good marsh ditch sites for 'bossing for ells', as Percy would have described it. (Photos by AL).*

in there. He often had dogs with some ailment. It was near the gate which came alongside the 4ft. wall dividing Andrews' big farm yard. Alec Bate's groom, Edwin, had a saddle room in the opposite corner from the back kitchen door. It was a dark night on Saturday at about 6 o'clock when about five of us were on the Bruck Stone and Alec Bate passed us in his trap going towards Sutton Weaver.

They said: "Now, Percy – the Black Hen!"

I said: "You all stop here," then I went and opened the loose box door, not thinking about any puppies, struck a match, then climbed up a ladder on the side of the wall. When I got up the loft I kept striking matches. Just as I found the Black Hen and pushed it up my waistcoat I heard Mrs. Bate shouting: "Edwin, Edwin!" and she was just holding the loose box door when I dashed out and knocked her over in the rush. Just then Edwin picked Mrs. Bate up. I was with my pals very shortly after and went over Andrews' wall with them with the Black Hen still up my waistcoat.

Edwin came dashing past, calling: "Police, Police!"

We shouted: "What's the matter?"

He got the Police and we said: "No one has passed here, we have been here about an hour."

Edwin said: "I know it is none of you."

Jimmy got his Black Hen and cut her wing so she would not go there again.

*

We used to have some good fun fishing for ells, especially after a thunderstorm. We went into the marsh ditches what we called 'bossing', we used to thread a bunch of worms on

● *A bridge on the marshes, where Percy and his friends were so at home. (Photo AL).*

● *The impressive entrance to the Drill Hall, Main Street, Frodsham, built in 1901 for the local Territorials. The carved inscription over the door reads "1 COMPANY 2nd E.C. V.B. C.R." which stood for 1 Company, 2nd Earl of Chester's Volunteer Battalion, Cheshire Regiment. In the 1890s they were commanded by Capt Harry Harrison and Sgt Thomas Evans was the drill instructor. (Photo by AL).*

worsted about 7 yards long, wrap them round our fingers then slip them off in a bunch and tie them tightly with string. We used a stiff rod about 6ft long and the string was about 6ft, then we'd go in the main ditches. You did not wait long for a bite and sometimes as many as six at a time would cling to the worms until you shook them off. I have known them bite so quick I have had three men busy putting them in buckets. They would bite so keen I thought their teeth must get stuck in the worsted. It is great sport, bobbing for ells.

I sometimes would have an umbrella opened and pegged upside down tied to stake to throw them in until I had got as many as I wanted. A large umbrella was very handy if you were where the grass was longer. If it was going dark they seemed to bite better in the dark. You never used a float, you always felt them tugging at the worms.

※

There was about nine boys in our gang, one named Joey Ainsworth was almost twice as big as any others – he joined the Volunteers when he was 15, and told them he was 18. They had not a helmet to fit him he had such a large head; they had to measure him for a helmet.

We were having a Hot Pot Supper at the Town Hall one Saturday night, and I sat next to Joey (I was then bugler in 2nd. Battalion Cheshire Volunteers). He had eight soup plates of Hot Pot, and I said: "Everybody's finished but you," but he did not mind. He said: "It was very good."

We went over to the Commercial Hotel after to have two Lemon Dashes. He said: "I won't be long" and went to the

● *This is a boxing match in the Frodsham area with a referee, c1890s. Percy enjoyed "a real good fight" with other young men on an unofficial basis, but (like little boys in the playground) they stuck to a strict code of conduct. (Photo reproduced by kind permission of Frodsham & District Local History Group).*

● *Helsby Station c1900. (Photograph reproduced by kind permission of Frodsham & District Local History Group).*

back. After about 10 minutes I went out and saw him vomiting over a large bowl.

He said: "I am coming now," then taking a red and white handkerchief out of his pocket he started picking bits of meat out of the bowl.

I asked: "What are you doing?" and he replied: "I am going to take this home for the cat."

$*$

I think this was the night after I had a real good fight with one of our gang called Jim Holland. He was tall, and we went to fight midway between Booth Street and Marsh Green Cottages opposite the Old Ash Tree. He knocked me down many times, made my nose bleed and gave me a fat lip, but after about half an hour he kept holding me. While he done this I was wiping my face on his, and we were both covered with blood. He gave in after about three quarters of an hour and we again became good pals afterwards.

I had many fights when working at the Helsby Cable Works. One night I was fighting a Fred Burkhill, a youth whose nick-name was "Weddy." We fought in the field by the roadside. He knocked me down many times and none of his pals would pick me up. Then Fred Tweedle came upon the scene.

I said: "No one will pick me up."

He said: "I will, if he knocks you down."

I think he only knocked me down once more. I hammered him for about ten minutes after that when he said he had enough and gave in, beaten.

Later I fought a man called Bob Purr who had a reputation

● *Helsby village in the early 1900s.*
(Postcard from AL's collection).

● *Hillfoot, Overton Hill, Frodsham pictured around 1911.*
(Postcard from AL's collection).

of having travelled with a Boxing Show for two years. He was 6ft. tall but thin. We decided to fight in Sam Peacock's orchard adjoining the Cable Works at dinner time. He had a long reach and knocked me down many times, always punching my face or head. After about half an hour he says: "Shall we have a wind?"

I said: "No, we'll fight till the five minutes to one buzzer blows then start again when we knock off work tonight."

I think these remarks made him lose heart. We clinched and I gave him many sharp quick jabs in his ribs, and a few minutes before the five to one buzzer blew he said: "I have had enough."

I said: "Be here at a quarter past five and we will start again."

He replied: "No, I have finished."

✳

I had not been living in Helsby long. I used to do lot of fishing and shooting then – it would be about 60 years ago. I caught lot of Tench in June. I used to go out at daybreak and one good place was Mr. Fletcher's ponds at Abbots Clough Farm, a place between Helsby and Manley where old monks lived hundreds of years ago. I used to get many over 3lbs. weight and the largest was 5lbs. I also caught Roach, Dace, Ells and would often take my gun when going fishing. One day I saw a cock pheasant run behind a fallen tree and squat in bunch of nettles growing beside it. I went the opposite way round and grabbed him, then screwed his neck and came back home. I had never had my line out! Another time when I was out with my rods and gun I saw a head of a big ell about 3 inches

MANCHESTER SHIP CANAL

● *The Manchester Ship Canal was constructed using 'state of the art' Victorian machinery and the muscle-power of 16,000 navvies. (Photograph courtesy of Cheshire Record Office).*

Frodsham has witnessed the construction of three major transport arteries over the past 100 years: the M56 motorway in the 20th century, and the Manchester Ship Canal and the Birkenhead Line railway in the 19th century.

The Ship Canal was built in response to the draconian tolls and harbour dues charged by Liverpool docks, which exercised a stranglehold over Mancunian trade.

In 1882 Daniel Adamson, a leading local industrialist, called a meeting to form the Manchester Ship Canal Company, to build a waterway and docks that would allow deep sea shipping direct access to the city. After three attempts, permission was granted by Parliament in 1885 to construct the canal and work began in November 1887.

One of the greatest and most ambitious engineering projects of Victorian times, it was eventually to cost £15m – nearly triple the original estimate. It suffered the usual financial crises inherent in such a scheme, and had to be bailed out by Manchester City Council, but was also fraught with many practical problems such as boggy ground and flooding caused by bad weather.

Major engineering feats were necessary to deal with the

continued p44

out of the mud only about one foot from the side of the pond, and the water was only about 3 inches deep. I put No.4 shot in my choke barrel, put the gun few inches from the water, allowing few inches below the ell's head. I fired and out come the wriggling monster, splashing. His head was almost blown off and he was three pounds in weight.

I have sometimes shot a couple of rabbits, caught a few fish and had mushrooms and watercress – a real mixed bag. I remember some years when I had been playing truant from school I found a lovely bed of watercress with leaves as big as a penny. I sent it to my mother before teatime. We had two lodgers then, working for the Manchester Ship Canal Co.. They had this for tea and next day at teatime they said it was beautiful and that they would like it several times a week. They asked me where I had got it from, and when I told them out of the big drain where all the drainage came out of the Churchyard of Overton Church, they then said they did not want any more and would not have had it if they had known!

✳

One of the strange shooting incidents I had one night after working till half-past 8. There was a lovely full moon and I then lived at Stonehouses, Robin Hood Lane. I was getting my gun from above the fireplace mantelshelf, when my father, who was smoking his old clay pipe by the fireside, said: "What are you going to do with the gun?"

I said: "I am going shooting," and he replied: "I never heard tell of anyone going shooting at a quarter to 9 at night."

I went down Robin Hood Lane towards the marshes, over

MANCHESTER SHIP CANAL continued

● *A land dredger. (Photograph courtesy of Cheshire Record Office)*

railway lines crossing the canal, as well as the construction of the Barton Swing Aqueduct for the Bridgewater Canal and the Swing Road Bridge at Salford Quays.

The contractor Thomas Walker used the latest equipment: 100 steam excavators, 7 earth dredgers, 6,300 railway wagons, 173 locomotives and 124 steam cranes.

Thousands of men and boys with spades and wheelbarrows were employed as labourers on 'The Big Ditch', as it was known, together with stonemasons, carpenters, bricklayers and other craftsmen. Their wages alone cost more than £1m. Many lived in temporary shanty towns along the canal, while the better-off among them – like the managers involved in building the railway some years earlier – lodged with local families like the Youds.

The work was dangerous and a pioneering accident service was set up. It comprised a chain of first aid stations and three temporary timber-built hospitals, strategically sited along the canal and supervised by a Liverpool orthopaedic surgeon.

The 36-mile canal, from Eastham to Salford, was built sufficiently large to enable ships capable of travelling anywhere in the world to reach Manchester – on the same principle as the Suez Canal.

Six locks were installed to raise the ships some 60ft 6ins. The first, at Port Sunlight, connected the Ship Canal to the

continued p46

the railway crossing alongside the railway, where a large flash of water runs from the crossing to Helsby Railway Station. In the join with the Birkenhead Railway and the Chester to Warrington line there is a "V" shaped 5-acre plot of waste land and it was there that I saw a heron rise. It was a big bird so I took a shot at it and killed it. It fell about one yard from the edge of the water where a hedge runs along, dividing the railway bank from the water. I then saw something swimming about 5 yards from the marsh side of the flash. I thought it might be a waterhen so I put up my gun and fired my second barrel. I intended to pick up the heron later but I had a shock for the thing I had shot at was spinning in a small circle. I reloaded my gun and went to look what I had shot. I was at least 50 yards from my object when I shot, when I got opposite to where it was just going round in circles, I thought I had shot someone's Irish Terrier. I went to break a bough of a large bush near the fence, and when I hauled it in I got a pleasant surprise. I had shot a large hare: the report of my first shot must have frightened it. It must have been sitting on the rough bank and taken to the water to swim the ditches as they are called. I was in a hurry to get home so after going to collect my heron I put the hare under my coat and was home in 10 minutes.

I said to my dad: "What do you know now about night shooting," so he said: "Anybody can shoot a heron, they are so big and slow."

Then I pulled out the hare and said: "But what about this?" and when I told him how it had happened he said he had shot a hare swimming when the tide was in at the Hopper Gutter, a big tidal water running into the River Mersey from the Helsby Marshes. It had taken to the water after being chased by a dog.

MANCHESTER SHIP CANAL continued

● *Setbacks were common when landslips or flooding occurred. (Photograph courtesy of Cheshire Record Office)*

tidal channel of the River Mersey and acted as a control stop-lock, so that vessels moored above the lock could remain afloat even when the tide was out.

With cargo-handling points along its length the waterway was virtually a linear port.

The Ship Canal was opened on January 1, 1894 when a flotilla of boats sailed the full length, and Queen Victoria later performed the formal opening ceremony on May 21, travelling on the yacht *Enchantress*.

● *A fine merchant sailing ship on the Canal at Eastham in the early years after its construction. (Postcard from AL's collection)*

I told some of my pals about this unusual event with the gun, so we had a good talk which ended in a 10/- bet that I could not shoot three rabbits in full moonlight after midnight any suitable night. Some weeks later when it was full moon and the snow was about 6 inches deep we played cards, Nap, about four of us until 12 o'clock midnight then we set out to settle the bet. Only I had a gun. We had gone along the back lane towards the hills to where Alvanley Road joins with Back Lane when a rabbit ran towards the hill. I shot twice and hit him and we found fur off him but he got away.

I said: "Better luck next time."

We went about a mile going towards the Keeper's Cottage, Dick Tweedle's, when I saw two rabbits about 50 yards from the fence. They ran towards their holes but I killed both with one barrel each. We then went towards Fox Hills. I killed two more there, then on towards Delamere Forest and I eventually killed seven rabbits by 3 o'clock and won my bet.

*

I often went out before daylight to get to Delamere Forest just as it was breaking day then went sometimes toward Fox Hills and the Royalties then zig-zagged towards Alvanley and Manley to finish at Helsby with 10 or a dozen rabbits. I always had a ready sale for them at 1/- each. My dad only had an old-fashioned muzzle loader and some nights he would ask: "Which way are you going in the morning if you go shooting?" I would sometimes tell him.

I remember one morning I had been to Delamere Forest and had a good bag. Coming back over Helsby Hill opposite the

● *The Robin Hood Hotel, Helsby.*
(Postcard from AL's collection).

● *Below: Chester Road, Helsby.*
(Postcard from AL's collection).

lake where there was an old marl quarry on the bend, I was creeping around the left hand corner when a rabbit jumped up, I shot him, and when I went to pick him up saw my dad just coming around the bend towards me.

I shouted: "Any luck?"

He said: "Luck be damned, I only had one shot and took a ruck of horse manure to be a covey (brood) of partridges and shot at that."

＊

He once said to me: "I will give you sixpence to fire my gun off," but I answered: "I would not shoot out of an old gun like that."

On the Sunday me and my pals were by the Robin Hood Hotel when a swan flew right over us going towards the marshes.

I said: "If he lets near the new ditches (Flashes Water) I will fetch the gun," although I'd never went shooting on Sundays before. I was only 150 yards from home, so I said to my dad: "I will fire your old gun, there is a swan just settled on the new ditches."

My pals followed 100 yards behind me, and when I got about 60 yards from the fence between new ditches and the crossing I saw the swan about 60 yards away. He had only just got on the wing when I shot, and the kick of the gun knocked me into the fence. When I was returning with the swan flung over my shoulder, just crossing the Chester Road, about 100 yards away was a lot of Chapel people coming. I felt so ashamed and hurried. When I got home my dad said: "Did the gun kick?"

THE SMELTING CORPORATION

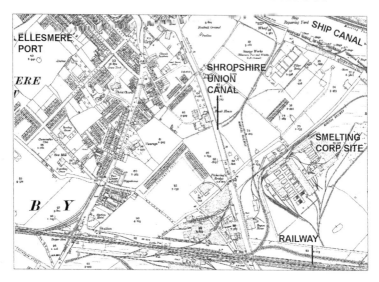

Going to work at the Smelting Corporation's new works in Ellesmere Port must have seemed a good career move for the ambitious young Percy. He was not to know that it was a doomed venture.

The corporation had been formed in 1898 to smelt non-ferrous ores such as silver, lead, zinc and gold, and experiments on a small scale at its Swansea works had proved encouraging. The company then acquired what it regarded as an ideal 60-acre site at Ellesmere Port on the Manchester Ship Canal, close to the Shropshire Union Canal terminal and beside the railway – excellent transport links for the time. Land was available for expansion, there was a good supply of labour and dwellings for workers could be built nearby.

The future looked rosy, although the corporation's new process had never been tried on a commercial scale.

What happened next is a tale of woe that will sound horribly familiar to many modern industrialists...

It was decided to start by building a third of the factory – but the project was only

continued p52

I said: "Yes, it knocked me against the fence."

He started laughing and said he was afraid to fire it off himself because he had forgotten that he had loaded it twice.

*

I went to work at Ellesmere Port in 1900 at the new smelting works and used to come home at the weekends.

One Saturday when I was coming up Station Lane, I met Dick Tweedle who said: "Your father has been fighting by the Horse and Jockey and he is in an awful mess."

I said: "It serves him right, he should not fight when he's drunk."

I lived in the opposite direction to the Horse and Jockey but I got to the top of Station Lane, was told again about my dad at the Horse and Jockey, and so I went. There outside with a bottle of pop on the window sill I saw my dad with an awful badly cut face and one eye swelled larger than his nose.

I said: "You do look a sight."

He replied: "I'm drinking pop to get sober. I was fighting Sammy Hibbert when Ben Inglesfield kicked me when I was down and I have offered to match you to fight any man within 20 miles for £5."

I said: "You haven't got one pound!"

I added: "Stay where you are," then went inside the pub and called for a glass of port.

My Uncle George said: "I will pay for that," but I said: "No Uncle, have a drink with me".

He said: "No thanks, I have just got one."

Sammy Hibbert was standing by the bar. I did not offer to

THE SMELTING CORPORATION *continued*

designed to make a profit when everything was completed. Only one director understood the technicalities of the process and no-one gave a thought to possible pollution problems.

Unfortunately due to miscalulations, the costs of materials, fuel and labour rose disastrously. By the end of 1899 only one of the two departments was working and a third of the plant operational. Hopes of overseas royalties on the corporation's patents were over-optimistic, too.

Construction of the cupola furnace was delayed until June 1900 due to mechanical problems. It was not set to work until July, and then not at maximum capacity.

There were difficulties with the company's ore supply and it had to look elsewhere for raw materials.

By 1901 the company was approaching liquidation, its problems compounded by the fact that the cupola furnace would only work continuously for two or three months at a time before it had to be be allowed to go out.

The process, when it worked, caused contamination by sulphuric acid and lead and gave Ellesmere Port the reputation of being a 'dirty' town.

The Dean and Chapter of Chester, and two farmers immediately adjacent to the works, applied for an injunction because they claimed the fumes from the factory were poisoning their crops and stock. The last straw came when a director was unable to pay the pledged £10,000 for his debentures. The official receiver was called in.

Later in 1901 the company was reconstituted and started to alter its plant to smelt copper. It then found itself in the midst of litigation for contravening the pollution injunction, which cost it £23,000.

From 1902 the firm staggered on, investing money in a Chilean company because it was now cheaper to smelt the ores where they were mined.

Once the town's biggest ratepayer, the Ellesmere Port works became a liability and the Smelting Corporation was finally liquidated in 1906.

In 1911 the site was taken over by a cement company.

touch my port but said that if I reckoned to be a fighting man I would never hit a drunken man or anyone who would not put them up.

He said: "Are you alluding to me?"

I replied: "Yes!"

He then said: "I'll knock your B. head off!"

The landlord Jim Jackson said: "Don't fight in here," so Sammy said: "Come out and get your rags off."

We went out with the crowd, and my dad said: "I'll hold your coat, lad."

I told him: "If I don't beat him without taking my coat off, I will never fight again."

Sammy stripped off until he only just had his pants on – he always fought with his shirt off. I knocked him all over the place and in less than half an hour he said: "Shall we have a wind rest?'

I said: "No, you are reckoned to be fighting man, we have not been fighting long enough for a wind," and about 20 minutes later he said: "I have had enough for today, will you meet me tomorrow Sunday at 8 o'clock?"

I said: "Yes."

We decided to meet at Rake Lane and shook hands. I said: "I will give you a real good hiding tomorrow," then went into the Horse and Jockey while he was getting his clothes on.

The Landlord said: "You have not drank your wine yet." Then he filled me one.

My Uncle George said: "Fill him one with me, Jim," and someone else called one. I had four glasses, but before I had drank a second one Sammy came in and said: "Perce, I am not going to turn up at 8 in the morning and I will never fight

HELSBY HILL RACE

● *Helsby Hill, whose profile resembles a face, pictured around 1910. (Postcard from AL's collection).*

Helsby Athletic Club was formed in 1895. Although it was independent of the cable company it had many employees on its committee and in its various teams. The club's first president was James Taylor, who held that position for more than 30 years.

The well-known Helsby Hill Race was always the last of the events to be run on the BICC Sports Day.

Though modern athletes would blanch at the thought of drinking eight small sherries before a race, the revolting mixture of raw egg and sherry was regarded as a regular "pick-you-up" in those days.

Percy's daughter Phyllis says that the last time she looked, Percy's carving was still on the tree at the bottom of the beech wood, where had had inscribed it.

But she says he had written his initials, "GTPY" and not his full name, as he states.

again."

He asked me to shake hands again which I did. I went to Prescot a few months after as a foreman for the Cable Works. From then until he died they say Sammy never fought again, and when I ever came over from Prescot we always had a drink together and were good friends.

✳

I won the Helsby Hill Race the following August, 1901. I had run third in 1899, but I did not run in 1900. I cut my name in the bark of a tree on the day after, just "P.Youd 1899". I saw it still there few weeks ago (1956) near where we ran past. I was running a trial on the Thursday night before the race on the Saturday: they stopped a cricket match and timed me. The record was broken for the second time by Fred Tweedle in 1899 from 8 minutes 25 seconds to 8 minutes 17 seconds, then I won in 8 minutes 16½ seconds which record still stands. My time on the Thursday night was 8 minutes 25 seconds.

The night before the race my mother said: "You are going with me to the Royal Infirmary at Liverpool to see your brother Fred, never mind the Hill Race. He has had a operation today, Friday, and you must come with me."

So I did, and the first thing he said was: "I had my operation yesterday: you go back and win the Hill Race."

It was then 3 o'clock. I said: "I am too late now," but he said, "It is not run till about 6.30 so get the first train from Lime Street, Liverpool to Helsby."

In them days not many trains stopped at Helsby, but they told me there was a train to Frodsham at 4.20pm so I got that

THE 'WIRE WORKS' AT PRESCOT

● *Architect's impression of the planned extensions to the British Insulated Wire Company factory at Prescot, c1902. The Imperial Hotel's roof and chimneys can be seen circled in the left-hand corner. (Photo by kind permission of Knowsley Museum Service).*

The British Insulated Wire Company was formed in Prescot in 1891 by James and Jacob Atherton, who acquired the British rights to an American patent for paper-insulated cables.

They chose Prescot because it had a labour force of skilled craftsmen, particularly in watch and tool making.

The firm expanded rapidly and soon a large percentage of the population was employed by the 'Wire Works'. At its peak the work-force numbered 10,000.

BIWC built an extensive industrial complex which cov-ered a large area to the south east of the town. It had its own transport system with roads and a steam railway to move supplies around the site.

The company subsequently became the British Insulated & Helsby Cables, then British Insulated Cables Ltd., and finally 'the BICC' (British Insulated Callenders Cables), which was the world's largest cablemaker.

Sadly, in recent years new technology and the introduc-tion of fibre-optics sounded the death-knell of the industry in Prescot – and Helsby.

and walked the 2½ miles to Helsby. My pals were delighted to see me and as I had been training on sherry I had eight small sherrys before going to run.

The Bookmakers were allowed to stand up, making a book. Jimmy Goodhall from Runcorn Tally Ho Harriers was favourite, he had been in the first three for seven years, so they shouted: "2 to 1 Bar Goodhall, 3 to 1 Micky Fallon" (a Widnes ½ mile professional). My odds were 6 to 1.

Before the start Jimmy Goodhall's brother was rowing with my pal George Warburton.

I said: "Don't you touch him, he's nearly drunk," so Jimmy then started on me. I said: "I'll thrash the pair of you in less than half an hour for a fiver when I come back."

The pistol went soon after and I went ahead with a sprint, they never caught me, I was first to the top of the hill and won easily by over 100 yards and the second man was over 100 yards in front of the third man, with Goodhall not in the first six – and I never met him again, only in a race. I had met him in a ½ mile race at Oulton Park on the Whit Monday 1901, he was off the 30 yard mark and I off 35. He asked me to make the pace, he said he wanted to win it. Me and Mountfield of Warrington were level at 50 yards from the winning post, and I looked around for Goodhall, but he had packed in so I jumped the tapes 40 yards from the winning tapes trying to get a bigger mark *[he tried to fiddle the handicapping system; Ed]*, got reported and a few weeks later at Connahs Quay was reduced to 20 yards, so I decided to give up running. This was my last time I entered for the 880 yards, in 1901. Fred Illes the North Wales all-distance runner was that day off the 15 yard mark.

✳

THE 'WIRE WORKS' AT PRESCOT continued

● *The cotton covering department building in Percy's day. (Photo by kind permission of Knowsley Museum Services).*

● *Women workers in the cotton covering shop, 1930. (Photo by kind permission of Knowsley Museum Services)*

I was sent to Prescot on Peace Day of the African War as fore-man of the Cotton Covering and Braiding Departments. Mr. Joe Crosland, then the manager of Helsby Cable Works, asked me if I would take the job. I could have double the money I was getting, was promised £1 week rise in 12 months, and he said I could always go back to Helsby if I was not satisfied at Prescot.

Soon after I went there was the Big Coal Strike and many families in Prescot suffered hardships as a lot of them were coal miners. The foreman of the Telephone Department and I arranged a Ladies' Football Match in aid of the Salvation Army Distress Fund for Miners – it was Cotton Covering v Telephone Ladies. I think this was the first Ladies' Match before Dick Kerr's. Soon after a notice was posted in each Department to say that anyone improving a machine or suggesting anything to increase the output or reduce the cost would be paid an award. I was No.1 on the list published (typed) and put up in every department. It read as follows: "Mr. Percy Youd has this day been awarded a sum of money for No.1 suggestion."

A Patent Compound Tank manager telephoned me at my office to ask me to come to the General Office Cashiers' Office to receive my award. I went and received five Sovereigns only. I later improved a German Cotton Covering Machine and got nothing. I ought to have had a few thousands for this and got nothing.

The manager rang me up one day to tell me that the Imperial Hotel opposite the General Office was becoming vacant and advised me go to Greenall's Brewery, St. Helens, to apply for it. He said: "You not need to leave our works", so when I went they said it was let but wanted me to leave my address. I told them the manager of the Cable Works at Prescot had sent me.

THE 'WIRE WORKS' AT PRESCOT continued

● *Percy should be here somewhere! The proud workers assembled for a massive 'group picture' in front of the new Insulating Rooms and the General Office, in the early 1900s. (Photo by kind permission of Knowsley Museum Services)*

● *Inside the insulating shop. (Photo by kind permission of Knowsley Museum Services)*

The following morning they wrote to ask me to come to see them and they offered me the Tenancy. I became the licensee of the Imperial in 1907 and got the Brewery to make a bowling green there. I was Treasurer of the Prescot Angling Society and also the Prescot Homing Club, and they both made the Imperial Hotel their headquarters.

I was President of the Prescot Football Club in 1914. I played a few matches for them in the Liverpool Combination. I also was well known in the Walking Races – 15½, 17½ and 18 miles. I got 6th in the first, I think there was over 100 starters, they gave three good prizes also a Gold Medal with each prize and 9 Gold Centre Medals, also a sealed handicap in the 17½ Mile Walk. Me and Bob Rodgers dead-heated for the sealed handicap so we divided it. In the 18 mile I got third, a lovely set of silver mounted carvers by Hall of Sheffield and a Gold Medal.

I raised a Rugby Team and played on the St. Helens Rugby Club Ground and we got beat by Varleys Iron Foundry 3 points to nil. They came to the Imperial to ask me play for St. Helens a week later but I refused.

I was bowling well after about 12 months and Jack Charnock the well known St. Helens professional challenged any in England for £50 with his novice. He used to often come to the Imperial Hotel them days. The match was made for me and Jack Charnock to play Billy Parr of Chatto Heath and Billy Mawdsley of Whiston, both County Players. There was a great crowd and we were losing 19-17, when Charnock said: "You lead the block, Percy." I led from the corner by the house to the far corner, about 2 yards on the green, we were two in. I shouted: "Be careful, Jack, we are two in that makes us 19 all." He came a bit too strong and knocked both my woods and we

THE IMPERIAL HOTEL

● *The Imperial Hotel, a typical large Victorian corner-plot public house, pictured around 1960. It now stands alone in the 'wasteland' of the demolished Cable Works, which is waiting for redevelopment. (Photograph courtesy of Greenall Whitley archives).*

The substantial Imperial Hotel stands on the section of Station Road, Prescot which was originally part of College Road before the cable works were built opposite. It is con-temporary with the railway station which faces it and was probably constructed just before Percy was born.

There are extremely frus-trating gaps in the records for known landlords and land-ladies. The first recorded landlord was William Mynett, from 1879-81. The names and dates are then: John Barker (1885-87), Harriet

Hannah Barker (1891-05), Percy Youd (1913-18), James Bryers (1924), Bert Green (c1945-6), Margaret Green (C1960s), Frank James Hampson (1978-81) and Daniel Patrick Denny (1987-).

One can only conjecture that when Harriet Hannah Barker left in 1905 the man-agers of the cable works decided that it would be a good idea to foster a 'recre-ation club' on the factory doorstep and came to some sort of deal with Greenalls. As a result they then asked

continued p64

62

were beaten. He nearly went mad and wanted to make another match, but I said "No."

✷

When the First World War broke out I joined up *[he would have been 35 years old; Ed]* and went away on the 15th November 1914. I was moved about a lot and never got to France. I was laid many months with acute rheumatics in Slimbridge Hall near Gloucester. I had been in 10 counties. When I was in Chester in early 1915 Colonel Cook phoned to ask the Captain to send Sergeant Youd over to St. Helens to raise No. 6 Coy. 215 South Lancs. I was offered a Commission in No.6 Coy. but refused. Captain Fearnley was O/C, Lt. Hall and Lt. Gandy who was up against me. We went to a village in Staffordshire to guard a bridge over the Trent at Armitage, but we were only a Detachment from the Company who were then at Oldbury. Lt. Gandy was billeted at the Vine Hotel at Stafford. I was the only Sergeant there with two Corporals, Lowe and Nolan. Gandy did not visit us too much, only by surprise. A Private named Dooley said to me: "Serg't I am going to shoot Lt. Gandy some night when he comes creeping on a night."

He came on a goods train one night, and got the driver to stop. Dooley told me: "I thought of shooting him." The goods train stopped near the bridge then he would get passenger train from Armitage back to Stafford. He came to visit the billets once so I told him.

He went furious, demanding: "What's the Private's name?"

I would not tell him, so he went to visit the Guard after and he said: "I will find out."

That same day Dooley was on Guard on No.6 post. He asked

THE IMPERIAL HOTEL continued

Percy, a trusted senior employee, to run it on their behalf because his family had experience of being licensees of the Cheshire Cheese (a Greenalls ale-house) and The Bear's Paw in Frodsham and of pubs in Ellesmere Port and Chester. The thinking amongst enlightened employers at the time was that workers should be enticed away from old-fashioned ale-houses – where they simply got drunk – and into public houses with additional leisure and sports facilities like those Percy persuaded the brewery to provide. He specifically says he was only the "tenant" until 1907.

● A trophy from Prescot Homing Club which had its HQ at the Imperial. (Knowsley Museum Services)

Indeed, since Percy continued to work at the factory for some years, it may well have been his wife Sally who bore the brunt of the day-to-day organisation.

● The Imperial Hotel (centre) showing its garden at the back and the bowling greens on the left-hand side. Various BIWC sports facilities were nearby. The station is opposite and the top of the picture shows the BIWC. (Photo by kind permission of Knowsley Museum Services)

each sentry from No.1 post to No.5, then came to Dooley.

"Did you tell Sergent Youd I came creeping to visit at nights?"

Dooley said "Yes."

Gandy screamed again: "Do you know who you are talking to? It's 'Yes, Sir!'" so Dooley said, "Yes Sir."

Gandy said: "I have a good mind to have you court-martialled," but I said: "Better forgotten."

＊

I had some good matches at bowls and other games, my best I think was a semi billiard with the Champion Billiard Player of St. Helens (Billy) W. Laycock who kept the Black Horse Hotel at Haydock. It was for £5 at the Imperial Hotel and drinks round, Game of 101 up. He won the toss and made 48. I went on and ran out first break, they asked me to finish my break, and I made 127. He was not satisfied so we made another match. He had the break again, made 56; I went on and won again and finished with 148 break. He then wanted a match at throwing at coconuts. At that time there was a big fair on a field 100 yards from the Imperial Hotel. We went to throw 100 balls each, and arranged with the stallholder for the loser to pay for the 200 balls. It was a penny ball and only one nut was placed for us to throw at. He went on first and only knocked 34, I won by getting 68, then I told him if he was fancying his chance with a catapult I would like to take him on, or with a marble shooting at a cork six feet away.

I used to keep all records of Sport – horse racing as well as boxing and fighting – and many bets were settled at the Imperial Hotel.

LOCK AH TAM

The following report was published in The News on Friday, April 23, 1971, written by Ken Whitmore in his series "Murders that made headlines":

NO MURDERER can have been more universally liked and pitied than Lock Ah Tam. Nobody had the slightest doubt that he shot his wife and two daughters at his home in Price Street, Birkenhead, in the early hours of December 2, 1925. But when he was sentenced to death 100,000 people petitioned to save him.

Respect for 53-year-old

● *Lock Ah Tam*

Tam was international. The money for his defence was raised by world-wide public subscription and bought the services of the country's most brilliant advocate, Sir Edward Marshall Hall, KG.

The voice of Mr. Justice MacKinnon at the trial at Chester Castle broke with emotion as he pronounced the death sentence.

Lock Ah Tam was an inscrutable Chinese, but not the one-dimensional figure of lurid fiction. For complexity of personality and romance of background, this penniless ship steward who suddenly appeared on the Liverpool waterfront in 1895 from the swarming obscurity of Canton, to become a merchant prince who slept with a revolver under his mattress, was a character fit to stride the pages of Conrad.

Witness after witness came forward to testify to his goodness, his integrity, his happy, loving family. "There is not a

continued p68

I had a grand collection of hundreds of stuffed birds, animals and freaks, including the largest two-headed calf in England, and a rat killed at Aspull near Wigan which weighed 15½lbs, was 36 inches long and was killed by a Pomerian Dog. This was said to be a record. They used to call it the 'Hotel Museum'.

I left Prescot when the 1914 war ended and went to Birkenhead, then to Ellesmere Port.

✳

I was a friend of the late Lock Ah Tam the Chinaman who shot his English wife and two daughters, Cecilia and Doris, after his son's 21st birthday party, about 30 years ago.

On the day it happened, he came to Ellesmere Port for me to go to Chester with him. He was a member of the Ellesmere Port Conservative Club. We went to Chester and I took him to a friend who kept the Pied Bull Hotel in Northgate Street. We had been to the Auction Mart Sale and bought some fowl, and we stayed talking to the landlord Albert Shrieff who had been in China for years, then we left about 5 o'clock.

When we got to Tam's house in Price Street, Birkenhead, Mrs. Tam said a feast would be ready in about half an hour, so we had a whisky, hot with lemon (Tam always had a Black & White Whisky as soon as we got in his house after we had been shooting or if we came from Liverpool or the Birkenhead Docks). He was the Chief who supplied all the Chinese Crews to the Blue Funnel Shipping Co. in Birkenhead or Liverpool.

We went over to the Westminster Arms Hotel, 100 yards from Tam's house, for about half an hour then went back home

LOCK AH TAM continued

more respected personality in the Chinese community on Merseyside," said Mr. John Shepherd, the prosecutor, in the early stages of the trial.

But, in the words of Marshall Hall, something took place which turned him from a kind, lovable, useful citizen into a raving maniac who butchered most of his family,

It all started so happily. There was champagne, whisky, beer and stout at the party in Price Street to celebrate the 20th birthday of Tam's son, Lo Ling Tam. There was dancing and singing, and when Tam toasted his son he made quite a beautiful little speech, wishing him success in the future.

Catherine Tam, who was shortly to be killed by a 12-bore shotgun fired by her husband from close range, added: "I hope Lo Ling Tam will grow up as good as his father has been."

The last guest left at a quarter to one. The son, in his third floor bedroom, heard his father enter his bedroom immediately below, and then the sound of shouting and stamping.

Lo Ling's sisters, Doris, 19, and Cecilia, 17, joined him and they rushed to their parent' bedroom, where they found their father, dressed in a nightshirt, in a violent temper with, their English mother.

Father and son exchanged heated words and the family was ordered from the bedroom. Mrs Tam and her daughters huddled nervously in a sitting room next to Tam's bedroom and the son went to the neighbouring house of the Chius, whose family owned the shipping company of which Tam was agent,

Margaret Sling, a 22-year-old orphan who had lived with the Tams for five years and been treated like a daughter, was ordered by Tam to bring his boots from the parlour and to get dressed. Passing his half-open bedroom door she saw, reflected in mirror, Tam holding a gun.

She rushed into the sitting room to warn the others and they barricaded the door with furniture. Tam knocked and demanded to be let in. When he went away they all ran downstairs to the kitchen.

continued p70

for the party to start in large room upstairs. Tam sat at one end with his eldest daughter Doris, who was about 18 years old, on his right, and me on his left; at the opposite end sat Mrs. Tam with their son Tommy on her right and Cecilia on her left, and about 20 guests sat at large table.

We started with Champagne. It was a grand party with turkey, chicken, fowl, pork, beef, vegetables etc., and all kinds of sweets. After each sitting we went downstairs, then into Ah Chew's next door, who was a assistant to Tam and a great friend. He had an English wife and two daughters. Tam's Chinese servant was a girl about 20 years old called Maggie Sing who went with Doris to the Empire Music Hall at Liverpool because Young Tam did not like Doris's boyfriend who had not been invited to the party.

I left about 10 o'clock. Tam said: "I will see you tomorrow."

I was then in digs at Hollybank Road, Woodlands, Birkenhead and used to travel from Birkenhead Town Station at 7.55am. When I got to the station platform just before the train arrived a commissionaire and two friends said: "Mr. Youd, your friend Lock Ah Tam the Chinaman has shot his wife and two daughters last night after a party!"

I could not believe them. I said: "I was at the party!" but as the train started the commissionaire showed me the *Liverpool Courier* and in the 'Stop Press' I saw the sad news. I did not know what to do but thought the Police would soon come to see me. I waited until noon then got a train back to Birkenhead. I thought I would call to see Ah Chew next door to Tam's house at 122 Price Street, but on my way I called at another friend's house, Mr. Denny, who had been also at the party. He was too upset to tell me so I went to Ah Chew who said that

LOCK AH TAM continued

It was there that Tam cornered them. Lo Ling and Mrs. Chiu, hearing screams, had come into the house and now saw Tam, gun in hand, following his wife down a passage leading from kitchen to scullery.

"He was frothing at the mouth and his eyes looked as though they were coming out of his head," said Mrs. Chiu.

Tarn shot his wife, then Cecilia.

Doris, hiding behind the scullery door with Margaret Sing, cried: "Oh, Maggie, isn't it awful! Do save me! Oh, daddy, what did you do it for?"

Tam pulled the scullery door open and shot Doris twice with a revolver.

Then he went into his office to telephone the police – and put away his guns.

When the police arrived, Tam greeted them with: "Come in, officers. I have done my wife in." A sergeant noticed he was calm enough to light a cigarette with one match.

Mr. Chiu arrived and Tam, speaking in Chinese, told him: "I am in trouble. Look after the business and do your best. If I get hanged get my body out and bury me by my wife and daughters."

On the way to the police station, Tam told the officers: "The trouble is through my son. My wife hasn't got a good word for me. My son is the cause of it all."

Tam never elaborated on this, but it was the only vestige of a motive mentioned throughout the proceedings. "The strong affection existing between the mother and son undoubtedly has some effect on the prisoner's mind," said Mr. Shepherd.

Percy Youd, organiser of the petition to save Tam, recalled at the trial that a few weeks before the murders he and Tam had been leaving the house when Tam told his son to look after the fire while they were away. It was out when they got back, and the son told Tam: "I am not here to look after the fire."

Lo Ling's constant companion was a youth named Ah Foo. The two frequently visited theatres and dances.

"You and Ah Foo kept late

continued p72

Tam had gone to bed when he heard rowing going on downstairs between his son Tommy and his sister Doris. Tam came downstairs in his dressing gown and said: "If you don't make a less B. row I will shoot the lot of you!" Mrs. Tam said: "Shoot me first!" and no sooner said, then he shot his wife. But only seconds before he shot her, his son, young Tommy, ran out of the back kitchen into the yard and picked a large jardinere containing a large aspidistra plant, and threw it through the window. Then he shot the youngest daughter Cecilia, then his eldest daughter Doris, who was not killed outright but badly wounded and died two weeks later. I went to their funerals. Tam rang up the Police few minutes after the tragedy and told them to come and lock him up as he had shot his wife and two daughters. He was a big strong man aged 52.

I was summoned as a witness for the trial which took place at Chester Castle. I was asked by some of the leading Chinese about getting a good defence. At that time Sir Marshall was a great man for defence so he was leading Counsel for the Defence with John Grace as Junior Counsel as he was President of our Ellesmere Port Conservative Club, and Tam was a Member. I forget if it was just before or after this time that John Grace became an MP. It was a two days trial; Tam was found guilty and sentenced to death.

I got a Magistrates' Order to visit him often and we got up a petition for a reprieve for him, but it was dismissed. He had done many kind actions for the poor and more than once when we were going to his house he said: "Look at them poor children, no shoes or stockings on a cold day like this," called them and took them to a shop and bought them shoes and stockings and gave them money also.

LOCK AH TAM continued

hours about four months ago, did you not?" asked Marshall Hall. "Yes, sir."

"There had been trouble between you and your father?" "Yes, sir."

Was Tam drunk at the party? None of those present thought so, although Margaret Sing, who danced with him, said he was a little intoxicated.

His son said Tam had been drinking heavily, but that signified little in a man who, according to the evidence of a senior Liverpool detective who was a regular drinking companion, consumed one and a half to two bottles of whisky every day.

Tam's craving for drink played a key part in the defence mounted by Marshall Hall.

In 1918 Tam was struck on the head with a billiard cue in a fight with two Russian sailors. Characteristically, this man who frequently assisted the law in tracing deserting Chinese sailors, was helping the police at the time.

After the blow on the head he drank more heavily and witnesses said that if contra-dicted he became practically lunatic at times.

"He seemed irritable and excited and stamped his feet at the least provocation," said the secretary of the Liverpool Chinese Republic Club, of which Tam was chairman.

"In his eyes there was a venomous look. Once I saw Tam stamping his feet and foaming at the mouth. After fits he seemed to know that he had done something wrong and would apologise."

Then, in 1924, Tam suffered a financial calamity, lost £10 000 in shipping shares and went bankrupt. After that he became more morose and drank even more heavily, said his detective friend.

Now Marshall Hall brought forward his star witness, Dr. Ernest Reeve, to declare: "In my opinion the wound Tam received from the Russian sailor might lead to a gradual deterioration of his mental and moral character. It might lead to a craving for alcohol and might also lead to epilepsy, which might be brought to the surface by drinking habits. I have come to the conclusion

continued p74

72

I have said to him: "Tam, you should not do that, their parents may be drinking and they may pawn the kiddies' boots."

So he replied: "I am sorry for the kiddies – they cannot help what their parents do."

He was a very careful man when out shooting. We had several shoots, and his favourite was Carlett Park, Eastham. Once when he had invited a Liverpool gentleman over for a day's sport, we had not been there very long and were starting near the old quarry. I put the ferrets in and soon a rabbit bolted. Sinnet and Tam fired two barrels each, then I shot and wounded the rabbit. Mr. Sinnit reloaded. I said "Don't shoot again." The rabbit was jumping about when Sinnit ran and struck at the rabbit to hit it with the butt end of his gun. He had hold of the gun with the barrels when it went off and I was just behind. It blew part of my pocket away and he broke the stock of the gun. Tam cursed him very much, gave the shooting up for the day and told him he would never be allowed again to come shooting.

The day before he was hung at Walton Jail, Liverpool, I thought I would go to see him for the last time. It was about noon on the Monday when I went. He had been in Hospital all the time he was awaiting his doom, and when they brought him into the room where I was he shook hands with me, a Warden on each side and the Chief Warden standing.

He said: "Did you get my letter this morning?"

I said: "No."

Tam said: "I wrote to you last night, I will write to you again tonight. How is your Mother and Father?"

I said: "All right, all right, thank you."

He said: "Thank all the people who helped with the petition

LOCK AH TAM continued

that this man was suffering from epileptic automatism."

Marshall Hall, conducting his last case, put it more positively: "The condition of mind he was in following drink brought on an active acute epileptic attack. In law, that means you should return a verdict of Guilty, but insane."

But after only 15 minutes, the jury pronounced "Guilty."

There was an appeal, but it failed.

Why did 100,000 try to save him?

His donations to charity were a byword. Walking up to poor children he would give them half-crowns. His guests were always assured of the utmost hospitality. Percy Youd, in a telegram to Walton Gaol on the eve of the execution, wrote: "Goodbye Mr. Tam. You are the best Chinaman that ever lived."

Stories that he was a secret society agent, that he was held in awe by all Chinese visiting Liverpool and dealt swift and stern punishment on those who defied him, were ridiculed by his friends.

The night before he was hanged he told a friend:

"I didn't know at the time that I was doing wrong. The Bible say when a man dies he goes to Heaven among his family and friends... I will be in Heaven tomorrow with my wife and daughters, whom I loved so much."

After the execution (described by the governor as skilful and decorous) a relation of Catherine Tam handed a bunch of daffodils to a warder to place on his grave. Even those most hurt had forgiven him.

and give them my kind regards, tell them I shall meet my wife and daughters at 8 o'clock tomorrow. I believe in the Bible, I am not a heathen although a Chinaman. You knew I loved my wife and daughters and if I had been in my right senses I would not shoot those I loved best, but the law is the law and I will go to my doom like a soldier, I shall not have to be helped to the scaffold."

The two Warders were both shedding tears with bent heads, the Chief seemed all right and I was standing the strain well when the Chief said: "Time's up," so when we shook hands I said: "Goodbye Tam, God Bless You – the best Chinaman that ever lived, I shall always remember you."

When I got back to Lime Street, Liverpool, I felt very much upset and went into the Post Office down the steps under the North Western Hotel. I asked an elderly man if I sent a Telegram to Walton Jail could he guarantee it would be delivered.

He said: "Yes, if you register it, it costs 2d only to register it."

I said "Thank you" then got a Telegram form and wrote "Goodbye Tam God Bless You best Chinaman that ever lived, I shall always remember you (Percy Youd)."

When I gave the man the Telegram he asked: "Do you know this man?"

I said: "Yes, I have just been to visit him, I have been a good friend."

He said: "It's a shame – this man should never hang, me and my wife was up till one o'clock this morning talking about Lock Ah Tam. The Home Secretary should be ashamed of himself."

Next day, Tuesday, I was auctioneering in the large shed in

LOCK AH TAM continued

The Ellesmere Port Pioneer carried the following report in its "Between Ourselves" column on February 12, 1926:

LOCK Ah Tam, who was sentenced to death at the Chester Assizes last week, was a wellknown figure in Ellesmere Port.

Being a close friend of Mr. Percy Youd of the Westminster Road Salerooms, where he often visited, he paid many visits to the town.

He was also a member of the local Conservative Club where he was well respected by all the members who came into touch with him for his genial and cheery disposition.

He accompanied the local Conservatives when they went to Llandudno last summer for the club's annual trip.

Westminster Road, Ellesmere Port, next to the Conservative Club. When I arrived there at 8.45am the flag at the Club was flying at half mast for Lock Ah Tam. I received the two letters from him after he was hung.

He had a brother Lock Ling Tam in Canton. Lock Ah Tam asked me to go over to China for a six-month holiday and said he would pay all expenses. He went to sea when he was 10 years old as cook's boy and was very ill-treated. He once asked me what I thought of an idea of his of exporting fish to China. I said: "I have seen the fishing boats at Peel, Isle of Man, bringing plenty of fish into Peel," so he said: "We will go over to Peel to see if we can get suitable premises and buy a few trawlers."

He sent his Secretary, a Chinaman named Mr. Ah Wee, who spoke very good English, a week in advance to enquire for hotel accommodation for us. We stayed at the Peel Castle Hotel. He had phoned Tam to say he had promise of a suitable place near the Docks. He took his car and driver, also his son Tommy and two other Gentlemen. When we saw the place I said: "Tam, the rent is too high and the fishing season here is only about four months in the year," so he said: "We will not go on with the idea but stay and have a holiday."

We went in the car to places all over the Island and one day he hired a boat to take a party fishing, about 12 Guests staying at the Peel Castle Hotel. He paid the owner of the boat £6 to take us five miles out beyond Peel. The boatman found fishing lines. We anchored about five mile opposite Peel Harbour and had a 1/- sweep for first man to catch. Lock Ah Tam won the sweep with a 5lb. Pollock – they are just like Cod Fish but nearly black.

We were having grand sport for about half hour when a very

● *Wild-fowl in flight over the marshes, painted by Harold Elsegood*

● *The ruins of medieval Ince Manor moated grange, once owned by the Benedictine Abbey of St Werburgh, Chester, and now standing in the shadow of Stanlow Oil Refinery. King Edward I visited in 1277. (Photograph courtesy of Cheshire Record Office)*

strong gale arose. He asked them to go below, they were near-ly all sea-sick and Tam had taken a few bottles of Black & White Whisky, Tam's son Tommy was lying helpless on deck while me and the Skipper was trying to haul the anchor. Skipper said "This is the worst gale I have ever been in." He told me try and get Young Tom below or he might well roll overboard. He was almost washed over the side of the boat when I grabbed his legs and rolled him near to the steps and shouted to his father to give me a hand to get him below. The gale abated and me and Skipper were very pleased when we managed to get the anchor up. He told me when we were struggling with it: "Look, we will have to try to swim it."

I said: "Five mile? Not me, I shall go down quietly."

I have often thought the tragedy would not have happened to his mother and sisters if I had let Tommy go over the side.

✳

We were once going on a shoot to Ince; we had small party of two cars. When we got to the Shrewsbury Arms Hotel, Mickle Trafford, we thought of having just couple of drinks. There were about six Gents in there with Setter and Spaniel Dogs. They got talking to Tam and said Mr. Ernie Hassel, a farmer, one of their company, will shoot a match with you for £5 best out of six birds.

Tam said: "I am not a good shot but I will make a match for Mr. Youd my friend to take anyone of you for £10 or £50 to shoot at 12 birds each."

So it was decided to shoot a match the following Wednesday for 12/6 Champagne Dinners at the Shrewsbury Arms Hotel.

● *Above and below: The marshes around Ince where Percy liked to shoot. (Photos by AL).*

Mr. Amos, the landlord, agreed to be referee, and we were to shoot behind the Hotel in one of his fields. The farmer lived about 100 yards from the Hotel. We were to shoot at 12 birds each. We came the following Wednesday, me, Tam, and four more pals. We were in two cars and arrived at 2 o'clock, the time arranged, but we were in for a surprise – there was only one man standing at the bar. We ordered our drinks and I asked the barmaid where were the gentlemen who were here last week. She nodded for me to come to the bar door to tell me the shoot was off as the Police had got to know and it was illegal to shoot pigeons out of a trap.

We only had about two drinks and said we were going to our shoot at Ince a few mile away. We asked the man at the bar but he politely refused, and we said we might call coming back about 5.30pm. So we did and was surprised to see the same man still there. We got our drinks and asked him again to have a drink.

He said: "Yes" and looking at me said: "I think I have met you before somewhere."

I said: "I don't think so."

He then said: "Did you play football?"

I said: "Yes, but it is many years ago, my last football match was against Garston Gas Works in the Liverpool Combination. I played for Prescot Wire Works (Cable Works) about 20 years ago."

He said: "Yes, I remember. I played for Harroby."

I said: "I left Helsby in 1902 and went to Prescot."

He said: "I live at Helsby and am retiring soon. I am a Police Sergeant and came here expecting to get a case."

We had a few more drinks and thought ourselves lucky the

● *Wildfowler on Frodsham marshes. (Photograph by kind permission of Frodsham & District Local History Group)*

● *Percy (second right) and his brother Alec (far right) pictured with their victorious bowls team – date and place unknown.*

shoot did not take place.

✳

Me and Tam had a very funny thing happen when going to shoot in Wales. A grown pig was killed when it ran under the wheel of my car. The farmer came crying and said: "Why did you not stop for my pig – it was worth £5."

So Tam said: "Well don't cry so much, I will buy the pig." He gave him £5 and the driver put the dead pig in the boot of the car. We had many a laugh at the way the farmer cried.

✳

I still carry Tam's visiting card he gave me with the address in Chinese on one side and his ordinary address on the other. He often came to Ellesmere Port to visit the Conservative Club.

✳

I played many matches bowling for £5, the first at the Conservative Club in Westminster Road was against J. Dean. I won 51 up game by 15, then I played an opening match at the Princes Hotel 51 up for £5 against W. Simcox. I won by 14 then played C. Price at the Conservative Club 51 up for £5, and won by 15. Then I played J. Slawson of Great Sutton for £5 31 up, I won 31-22 then played E. Nicholls at the Conservative Club 21 up for £2, I won 21-14. I played W. Simcox in the second match at the Conservative Club 51 up, I won by 15, then played W. Davies 21 up at Conservative Club at a fixed Jack corner to corner match for £1, I won 21-6. I played J. Slawson second match 21 up for £1, I won 21-7. I played my Brother Alec Youd for £2 on his own green at the Princes Hotel [Ellesmere Port; Ed]

Extract from **The Ellesmere Port Pioneer, Friday, 26th October, 1956 (at the time of the Suez Crisis):**

Foreign Secretary At Conservative Club
TREMENDOUS RECEPTION FOR MR. SELWYN LLOYD
Opens New Concert Hall

Britain's Foreign Secretary and Conservative M.P. for Wirral, Mr J. Selwyn Lloyd received a tremendous welcome when he visited Ellesmere Port on Saturday night to open a £15,000 extension to the Conservative Club in Westminster-road.

He was greeted at the entrance to the new building – a well-appointed and spacious concert hall – by Councillor J.W. Flather, the club chairman.

And as the Foreign Secretary entered the packed hall a trumpet was sounded by 77-years-old Mr. Percy Youd.

Among the platform party welcomed to the ceremony by Councillor Flather were the Mayor and Mayoress, Ald. H.G. Black and Mrs. A. Percival; Sir Robert Catterall; Col. Gordon Glover, M.P.; Mrs. J.W. Flather; Mr. L. Rutter and Mrs. D.G. Mellis; Mr. D. Smith (club vice-chairman); Mr. J.M. Harvey (chairman, Wirral Conservative Association) and Mr. J. Davies (club secrtary). Representing Messrs. Ind. Coope and Allsopp Ltd. were Messrs. F. Wiggins and H. Davies.

After Councillor Flather had warmly welcomed the guests, Mr. Lloyd was the first of several speakers to reply. Right away, he amused his audience by confessing that he was now having to deal with two canals!

He was trying to represent Ellesmere Port, a most important port on the Manchester Ship canal, he said, and considered that Col. Nasser and his tricks with the Suez Canal represented just an incident.

Mr. Lloyd congratulated the club committee on having completed the first stage of their scheme of extensions. He had always regarded the club as the backbone of his support in Wirral and he hoped that in planning further extensions the committee would have serious regard to providing a "home" for the 300 Young Conservatives in the town.

Mr. Lloyd made but a brief reference to international affairs. One of the things he had been trying to do over the past two months was to stick up for British rights, he said. What was more, he had been standing up for the rule of law and respect for international obligations on the part of other countries.

There would be no lasting peace in the world, he went on, unless the rule of law was observed, because if people went on breaking contracts and treaties and were not called to book it would be an unhappy and unpeaceful world for everyone.

The Mayor acknowledging the welcome to himself and the Mayoress, declared: "We all have confidence in Mr. Lloyd attending to the Suez Canal business on our behalf.

"I always recognise the capabilities of a good man, no matter what his political colour may be, and I feel certain Mr. Lloyd will do what is best for this grand country of ours."

Thanks to Mr. Lloyd, and to all who were associated with the work of the club, were expressed by Councillor Flather, seconded by Mr. Dan Smith, vice-chairman of the club, who also paid tribute to Councillor Flather's work as club chairman.

The opening ceremony over, Mr. Lloyd moved about the new and the old building, greeting numerous old acquaintances, and afterwards returned to the concert hall for a concert arranged by Mr. Jimmy Davies, who was also compere.

for £2, I won 31-14. He was not satisfied so we played another match, one at the Princes and one at the Conservative Club, 21 up aggregate to count. I won 21-6 at the Club and when we played at the Princes Hotel he would not finish the match after he could not win.

My greatest matches were when I beat Dick Lamas, Thatto Heath 21-0 for £25 and I beat Joe Bromlow pointless at Villa Marina I.O.M. and I have only been in last eight prizes once. I beat Morris Radcliffe in the Waterloo, Blackpool when he was favourite and won a match in the Professional Tournament at Squires Gate, Blackpool, when I played under name of 'Alf Jones, Ellesmere Port'. I played a few times in New Brighton Tournament but never got farther than the fifth round and never got more than the second round at the Talbot, Blackpool. I got beat by W. Simcox in the last match I played him for £5, by 51-47.

∗

I have not played for a few years now through rheumatics, sciatica and arthritis, and I am now only just able to hobble on two sticks.

I was an Auctioneer and Furniture Dealer in Ellesmere Port for a few years. All names given are correct and the stories are true.

I blew the General Salute for Mr. Selwyn Lloyd the first time he came into the Conservative Club when he was elected MP for Wirral and when he came to open the new extension costing £15,000 on October 20th, 1956. [*Percy had been a bugler in the Cheshire Volunteers before World War I; Ed*]. I have had two or three letters from him thanking me for chocolates sent to his

On Thursday, 3rd August, 1961, the Ellesmere Port Pioneer devoted its front page and a whole inside page to the opening of the £133,500 quarter-mile long Westminster Bridge by Selwyn Lloyd – by then Chancellor of the Exchequer. The 'second' main story on page 7, which mentions Percy Youd, reads (rather strangely in places):

POOR VIEW FOR STATION-ROAD CROWD

NO SOUND – EXCEPT BUGLE CALL

Crowds which gathered at the Station-road end of the bridge – and they were there in their hundreds – were first to get a close-up of the Chancellor as he arrived and they certainly had a good view as the cavalcade of vehicles made the hair-pin bend from Station-road, having passed over the level crossing and turned on to Westminster Bridge.

But that was where their priorities ended. The crowds surged forward in the wake of the parade following the Chancellor and gathered as near the brow* of the bridge as they could get, but they found themselves cut off from the official part of the ceremony.

The dais faced Whitby-road so that those on it had to turn their backs on the Station-road end of the town.

But the crowds waited patiently, thinking that when the speeches began they would be able to hear what was being said.

No such luck! Loud-speakers were turned in the direction of Whitby Road.

Certainly onlookers saw Mr. Lloyd cutting the tape formally to open the bridge, but apart from that they had a dumb-show, and from behind the scenes at that!

For the want of an extra loud-speaker the crowds, including many young people, missed this opportunity of hearing the Chancellor.

It was surprising that they did not lose interest, but humour saved the day, and they interspersed the speeches which were lost to them with "Here here's" in the best Parliamentary fashion.

There was, in fact, a lively welcome for the Chancellor on the Westminster-road.

To start with, there was the general salute sounded on a bugle by Mr. Percy Youd, of Grace-road, who was 82 on Sunday.

And Mr. Lloyd apparently appreciated this friendly gesture, for he turned round in his car to wave to Mr. Youd in acknowledgement.

Afterwards Mr. Lloyd walked back to where Mr. Youd was waiting, and there took place a little presentation ceremony: Mr Youd handed ...* Mr. Lloyd a china jug* as a day-late birthday gift for himself, and a Maori girl doll* as a gift to take back to his daughter, Joanna. (*These words are hard to read as the microfilm is very damaged).

As a social history footnote, we add the following quotes from the 'lead' story on this page:

During the days preceding the opening of the bridge, there were persistent rumours that Mr. Lloyd would not be coming to Ellesmere Port.

They stemmed from an ill-founded opinion that after announcing his Little Budget the Chancellor would be 'afraid' to appear.

Mr. Lloyd has faced sterner opposition than he might have anticipated on Saturday, and when he did arrive at the top of the bridge from Station-road side to mount a canopied dais, cheers of welcome drowned the few grunts of disapproval to which expression was half-heartedly given....

wife and their little daughter Joanna, aged 4. She has sent me two letters since Xmas 1956. I also had a letter thanking me for my suggestion from Sir Anthony Eden, in November 1956. I wrote to Stanley Matthews, Blackpool, and told him I had told Sir Anthony Eden that Mr. Selwyn Lloyd was our MP for Wirral and as he had done much good for the country, we would like to call him "Sir" Selwyn Lloyd. I said I hoped when the next Honours List came he would not forget him and the Blackpool International great forward Stanley Matthews. This letter was written on 19th October 1956. Sir Anthony replied a few days later thanking me for my letter and said he would bear my suggestions in mind. I was delighted to see Stanley Matthews in the New Year's Honours List as I had suggested.

A few weeks before this I was sitting by my fireside at Marsh Farm Cottage after 9pm when a loud knock came from my door. I had locked the door so I shouted: "Who's there?

A voice replied: "Friend."

I said: "You're not much of a friend to come this time of the night."

I unlocked the door and asked: "Who are you?"

He gripped me by the hand saying: "Don't you know me, Percy?"

I answered: "No."

He then said: "I am Bob Rodgers from Prescot."

I said: "I am delighted to see you, come in."

He said: "I am sorry I cannot come in as the car over by your pond is waiting for me."

I said: "Just have a drink – wine or rum?"

He said: "No thank you, I am off tomorrow to Canada on 12 months' holiday and it is over 50 years since we played foot-

SEVEN YEARS' BAD LUCK

● Left: Signed certificate for right of burial in Grave Space No. 55 in Helsby Cemetery

● Below: Receipt for interment of Leonard Youd, in Grave 55, £3 10s 0d

ball together when we won the Brigade Championship at Knockaloe in the Isle of Man, and don't you remember when we walked Dead Heat in the Prescot Big Walk, that's also 50 years ago."

I said: "Look at me now – job to hobble on two sticks."

He was a grand man. I said: "Give my kind regards to all at Prescot and God Bless you and your family."

I remember when I lost my favourite boy Len, who died suddenly, Bob Rodgers came to try and console me and came to the funeral at Helsby the day the King's horse Minoriou won the Derby.

I went nearly crazy, Len was such a lovely boy, aged 6½ years old. I had an awful spell of bad luck for seven years.

When he was only a small toddler he came into our coachhouse one Friday and saw me drowning some kittens. I was leaving one so he picked it up and said: "Here, Dad."

I said: "No, Len, we leave one to let the cat suckle."

Next day my wife had been serving in the bar at the Imperial Hotel when she was taken ill. I sent for the Nurse at 1pm. At 2pm the Nurse came downstairs said: "Twins, Mr. Youd. Beautiful boys, 6lbs and 5½lbs weight, come and see them."

Len said: "Can I come, Dad?"

I said "Yes," and when we got into the bedroom I said to Len: "Now we have two more little brothers for you, Len."

He looked at them and then said to me: "Are we going to keep them both, Dad?"

But 10 weeks later while the Nurse Girl was taking them in the pram about 100 yards from the Imperial Hotel, where Station Road joins College Road, she let them go off the Parapet and both tumbled into the road. She picked them up

SEVEN YEARS' BAD LUCK continued

● Above: Receipt for interments of Cyril Youd, £1 17s 0d, and Sidney Youd, £1 14s 0d in Grave 55, Helsby Cemetery.

screaming and put them into the pram then came to the Imperial Hotel with the twins bleeding and her crying. We telephoned for the doctor, and when he came he said: "I am sorry, one will go blind."

Later when they were 10 months old Cyril died, and Sidney got worse. The doctor then told me the child might live until 12 years old but would never walk or talk and was now going blind. We were very upset.

I said: "Doctor, if what you tell me is true would not it be better if the child died?"

I idolised this child and as he got older we got him an invalid pram. He was always lying down and grew fast. When I came home on leave from the Army he would start laughing aloud and kissing us. I learned him to, by smacking his lips and making a kissing-noise. He knew my footsteps if I had not been on leave for over six months. He was 6½ years old when he died but he never walked or talked and was blind.

✳

I had a simple accident that turned out awful. I trod on a nail sticking through the lid of a whisky case at the Imperial Hotel and ran it through my boot into my foot. It was Friday noon while I was off for a midday meal. I went across to Prescot Works only 50 yards away for an Ambulance Man to put iodine on and phoned for the Works Doctor who came down in an hour and said: "Just rest it and I will call and see you on Monday."

But the pain was awful all night so I phoned Doctor Youatt. He came and said: "Send up for a bottle of medicine."

I went worse and on Sunday I telephoned for another doc-

SEVEN YEARS' BAD LUCK continued

● *Map of Prescot taken from the Ordnance Survey of Lancashire and Furness, dated 1908.*

More than 80 years after the event, it is very hard to understand how the little Youd twins were so badly brain-damaged as a result of the tragic accident when they fell out of their pram.

The 'parapet' or kerbstone, must have been very high – maybe they fell on to cobblestones.

The Ordnance Survey map above, dating from 1910, shows how College Road adjoined Station Road. The Imperial Hotel is clearly marked opposite the station. The road layout is quite different nowadays, as College Road has disappeared and Station Road just has a dogleg in it at the old join.

● *This architect's impression (left) shows the pavements clearly – though the scale of the horses, carts and people is wrong. The 'parapets' also show up on aerial photos.*

tor, Doctor Green. He advised poultices and on Sunday night I got them to telephone Doctor Wild, who had come on the Friday. He got very annoyed when I told him I had had Doctor Youatt on the Saturday and Doctor Green on the Sunday.

He said: "Did you tell them I had attended you?"

I said: "No."

He said: "You are not supposed to have two doctors."

I said: "I did not know that."

He said: "You can have one and a specialist if you like and you must phone them and have either of them or me."

So I got them to phone them and kept on with Doctor Wild who was the Works Doctor and I was an honorary member. He ordered me to bed then used to put a lance into the wound every day. I had to have an arched frame over me so that the bedclothes could not touch me. I used to cross my hands behind my neck then grip the 2in. pillars of the brass bedstead and scream. It was awful painful – I had to have my leg on raised pillows two feet higher than my head. My foot went black and swollen larger than a football. I asked the Doctor to take my foot off at the ankle but he refused and few weeks later it had gone black to my knee, I said: "Take it off at the knee, Doctor!" but he would not hear me. I had gone grey after two weeks. I used to have black hair. I was going to a skeleton when my leg got bigger than my body and black almost to my hip. I said: "Send one of the servants to ask the manager of the Works, Mr. Bates, if I could have a car to take me to Royal Infirmary, Liverpool to have my leg taken off."

He said "Yes."

This was 9.15am on the Wednesday. I told them to phone Doctor Wild, who said: "He must not be removed as a

CONTEMPORARY SCENES OF PRESCOT

● *Boys wait to cross over the tram line in Warrington Road, Prescot, around 1910. (Photo from AL's collection).*

Prescot is an ancient town, believed to have Anglo-Saxon origins. In 1391 the manor was bought by John of Gaunt and on his death it passed to his son, who later became Henry IV. In 1447 Henry VI included both the manor and rectory of Prescot as gifts to establish a college at Cambridge University.

A number of fine Georgian houses were built in the town centre.

The town's first notable industry, dating from the 14th century, was the making of fine pottery. In the mid 18th century there were seven kilns dominating the landscape.

From the early 16th century, the rich coal seams in the area were being exploited.

Craft industries such as toolmaking and watchmaking grew up in small workshops, and in 1795 Prescot watches were said to be the best in the world.

The population mushroomed from 700 in the 1690s to 3645 in 1801. By 1851 nearly a quarter of the residents were Irish.

In the 18th century Prescot benefited when the local turnpikes were greatly improved.

The town got its first railway station in 1871 on the branch line between Huyton and St Helen's and its first tramlines in 1901, connecting it to St Helens and Warrington.

Specialist is coming from Southern Hospital, Liverpool, and they are operating on him at 12 noon."

So when they arrived, the Specialist said to Doctor Wild: "This man could not live until 6 o'clock tonight without an operation."

Doctor Wild said: "Have you brought your instruments with you?"

He said: "Yes," and when he had taken them out of his bag I said: "Doctor, you have brought enough instruments to cut a Battalion up."

He said: "We are not going to use them all."

They gave me chloroform on cotton wool but before they placed it on my face, I said: "Doctor, you can saw it off or cut it off and if you will be quick I will not scream aloud. Cross my hands behind my neck like I do when Doctor Wild gives me the knife," but the Specialist said: "Put this over your head and take deep large breaths."

It was a cotton wool mask that came down to my shoulders like a diver's helmet, and I was off.

That was half past 12 on Wednesday noon, they had opened my foot from toes to heel and taken two bad bones out of my foot. They had a very hard job to bring me round, they say they gave me up at 8 o'clock, when my heart had stopped beating; they then commenced again to smack me and just at half past ten I showed signs of movements and came out of my operation. They asked me how I felt with my leg off, and they kept on talking to me. After a while I asked for a drink of water, but they said "no".

The Specialist asked: "What time does the last train leave Prescot for Liverpool?"

CONTEMPORARY SCENES OF PRESCOT, cont.

● *Prescot railway station in around 1910. The Imperial Hotel, built at about the same time in the 1870s, is opposite the entrance (out of the picture) on the left, beyond what appear to be hoardings. The older Youd children remembered seeing World War I soldiers coming from the station, possibly on their way to the barracks in Prescot town. (Photo courtesy of Knowsley Museum Services).*

● *Eccleston Street, Prescot, around 1908.*
(Postcard from AL's collection).

My doctor said: "11.30 and the station's only few yards away."

The Specialist then said to my doctor: "If he lives till Sunday cross cut him on top of the foot and leave about an ounce of blood in him as a last resort. It is the worst case of blood poisoning I ever saw."

The following day Doctor Wild said: "I've got to take the small bandages out of your foot."

I said: "Give me chloroform," but he refused and I asked to have morphia but he again refused. They cut me over the top of my foot and took the bandages out, the pressure of blood was so strong it went across room on either side of the bedroom wall. They held my leg in very large bowl and blood and matter oozed out to fill two buckets. My leg had been larger than my body before he cut me.

I was many weeks before I was able to get about on crutches. The first time I ventured to the front door an old gentleman came and said: "I am thankful to see you; it is many weeks since my wife said Mr. Youd has had his leg taken off and they said he died last night."

A few months later my wife was seriously ill and we had to have a Specialist. We had lost two boys aged 6½ years *[Percy gets carried away with his repetitions of '6½ years' but the sums don't add up; he was obviously upset when writing this and didn't work it all out properly; Ed]* and one boy at 10 months.

✳

I used to have some Champion Show Dogs when I was at the Imperial Hotel and once had 15 at one time. In 1911 I had the Dalmatian Champion Ballette whose picture is in *Cassell's Book*

CONTEMPORARY SCENES OF PRESCOT, cont.

● Above and below: The former Lancashire Watch Co. factory off Warrington Road was used as a barracks for the 'Liverpool Pals', the 17th, 18th, 19th and 20th Volunteer Battalions of the King's (Liverpool) Regiment during the First World War. Watchmaking had been a major industry in the town, but the factory could not compete against cheaper American and Swiss manufacturers and closed in 1910. (Photos from AL's collection).

of the Dog and *Animals of the World*. She was the greatest of all Dalmatians; my other well-known winners were Puritan and Nydia. I had 10 Dalmations, Borzoi, Collies, Poms, eight varieties of Fowl, also Pigeons, Bantams, Goats, Pigs, Ferrets, Cavies and Rabbits. My best Rabbits were Flemish Giants, I had one shown at Stockport in the Championship Class of '28. It won 2nd. Prize, and was 17¾lb. weight. I had a Rose Garden of over 700 trees and won 1st. Prize at Prescot Show Open Class for Roses. I also won 1st. Prize for Tomatoes and a large crowd visited to see oranges grown in my greenhouse which came to full size and colour.

The great Prize Fighter Jim Mace came to see these not many month before he died. He was visiting the Wallaces who had a large fairground near the Imperial Hotel and we became very good friends. He told me he used to have a large hotel in Birmingham himself some years before. I had a donkey that died, and Jim Mace said he had never seen a dead donkey before.

※

I have had some bad luck also in Ellesmere Port. I used to be often having nightmares and one Sunday morning I said to my mother and father who were then living at 10 Wellington Road, Ellesmere Port: "Mother, I am sorry the bed is wet. I have had an awful nightmare."

She said: "What – have you wet the bed?"

I asked: "Did you hear me screaming?"

They had just finished breakfast about 9 o'clock.

I said: "I don't feel like any," but she said: "It's cooked, get it. Egg and bacon."

THE CONSERVATIVE CLUB

● *Conservative Club, Westminster Rd, Ellesmere Port, after erection of the concert hall in 1956. (Photo courtesy of Cheshire Record Office)*

Success against the Liberals in the March 1907 urban council elections prompted the local Conservatives to establish a workingmen's club in Ellesmere Port – previously a Liberal stronghold.

By February 1908, the party had 300 members and was was one of the largest and most active in the Wirral division. The new club's founder and president, Mr H W Boultbee, said there were "200 good sound Conservatives on the books and many more outside the club".

Besides various eminent figures, industrial entrepreneurs and businessmen, those holding the 10/- ordinary shares in the club included small traders, foremen, agents and labourers.

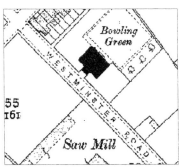

● *The club as it was when Percy first became a member. His auctioneer's business was on the land next door for a number of years.*

I said: "Oh, buried alive! I always said I would be buried in a trance."

She said: "None of your Conservative yarns here, you stay there every night till 11 o'clock listening to some yarns then try to tell us them."

I said: "No, Mother, it was awful, I thought I just woke when I found myself in a coffin and started to shout 'Save me! I am not dead yet!' but no one could hear me. I heard the sound of lumps of clay, stone and soil sounding on the coffin. While I was shouting and screaming but not heard, I then thought I might be able to scratch a way out of the coffin. After hours of agony and scratching my fingers seemed to wear off to my hands, I thought it must be a thick coffin and I am 6ft. below. I thought I heard sounds of digging then the coffin being hauled up then voices, then I heard voices and the doctor's voice saying 'He is dead enough' and heard my boy Percy say 'My Dad always said he would be buried alive', then I heard the Joiner say 'This is the last screw', so I lifted my hands up to show them I had scratched my fingers off and as they lifted the lid off my hands fell to bottom of the coffin and my eyes closed. I tried to speak but could not so the doctor said 'Screw him up again and bury him, he's dead enough'. I could hear all they said but could not move or speak. I heard them lower me again with a bump and then for the second time heard the stones, clay and soil sounding on the coffin."

I must have woken soon after. I did not enjoy my breakfast.

Mother then went upstairs and brought the sheets, quilts and pillows down to show my Dad who said: "Did you have any extra drink?"

I said: "No, you know I don't take much and I have never

THE CONSERVATIVE CLUB continued

● *Frustratingly, the first archived record of Percy playing a major role in the Ellesmere Port Conservative Club comes in a report of the AGM in the Pioneer of January 23, 1925, which has had part of the text cut out so that the newspaper's accounts department could have a copy of the advertisement on the other side of the page!*

Conservative Club
Annual General Meeting

...That the members of the Club are most jealous about the calibre of the Management Committee is demonstrated by the fact that each succeeding year the competition for positions on the committee becomes more and more keen.

occasion, although there was
ht seats vacant, eighteen cand-
h the result that the following
en were returned in the order:
.J. Rogerson, A. Davenport,
esley, T. Nicholas, H. Corbin,
e J. Jeffries, T. Thompson. In
other official vacancies Mr W.
y being appointed vice chairman
. Davenport a trustee, two
es were caused on the Commit-
ch were filled by the next low-
the ballot list, Messrs P. Youd
Davies.

been drunk."

When I went into hospital few years ago for serious operation, to have abscesses taken out of my stomach, I told Mr. Jack Dutton who saw me into the ambulance that they would operate on me same evening. He said: "No they won't." That was at 3.30 in afternoon; at 8 o'clock same evening the doctor came with a form for me to sign. I was in a special ward not far from the Operating Room, and he said: "Who shall we send for if things go worse?"

I said: "My Dad lives at the Princes Hotel with my nephew and niece and if it is midnight don't worry them, just let me pass out and tell them in the morning."

So then they wanted to carry me onto the operating table.

I said: "I can walk; it is only few yards just up two steps."

When I got onto the table and they tied my legs, one of the Sisters said: "Oh, your teeth – we must take them out!"

I said: "No, they are not false," and grinded my teeth and said: "These are my own."

They gave me a needle then I remember four of them carrying me and putting me into bed. I thought I was drunk and said: "Fancy that. I've never been drunk before and don't tell my Dad."

I had many visitors morning, noon and night, this is allowed when you're in a Special Ward. About week later the Matron who was kind and good said: "Mr. Youd, we have had a phone message to ask us if we would allow you to have dinner from Sportsman's Arms Bowling Club as it is their Annual Dinner tonight, so I asked the Doctor and he said all right."

So about 6.30pm Mr. Fred Hughes, a member of the Bowling Club, came with a fine dinner of turkey, pork, vegetables and

WESTMINSTER ROAD SALEROOM

● Advertisement in The Ellesmere Port Pioneer on October 7th, 1921 - the auction rooms exist but Percy doesn't seem to be involved

TOM BAIRD

Westminster Road Auction Room
Sale of furniture, etc.
Wednesday next, 2.30pm.

● Percy's first known advertisement in The Ellesmere Port Pioneer on April 28th, 1922. He appears to have a partner:

FRIDAY MAY 5TH
at 11 o'clock
Westminster Road, Ellesmere Port

YOUD and LEWIS

will sell by auction at their Saleroom as above a large assortment of valuable items briefly

Upright grand piano, chesterfield suites, display cabinets, drawing suites in plush, dining tables, bed chamber suites, walnut and ash chests of drawers, kitchen dressers, baby wringing machines etc. etc.

On view Thursday and morning of sale.
Further particulars from the auctioneers.

sweets, and a bottle of beer. He said: "Matron said we must ask the Doctor if you can have the beer."

I replied: "Let me have it now and ask him tomorrow!"

I had lovely good feed and few days later I told Sister and Nurse if I ever had a nightmare they should take no notice: I shout loud and may scream but I come quiet again later. The same night just after midnight I started shouting: "Oh, Oh, Oh!" and screaming aloud so that Sister and Nurse came to my Ward door. Just after I woke I heard one saying to the other: "You go and take his temperature," then a third Nurse came.

I said: "Come in, what are you afraid of? An old man, a 72-year-old!"

When they took my temperature, I said: "I was dreaming I was in Malaya [sic] and volunteered to go hunting Mau Maus, and we were in a forest and when I was going along a narrow path between two trees, two big black men grabbed me and took my rifle off me then stripped me, sliced a big slice of flesh off my leg and said: 'Steak!' Then another slashed a slice off my arm then turned me and sliced part of my bottom off, saying: 'Rump Steak!' I said: 'Cut my head off but don't torture me any more!'"

They thought it very funny and had many a good laugh.

∗

I remember years ago when I was licensee of the Imperial Hotel, Prescot after the Big Bowling, when me and Charnock were beaten 21-17, one of the winners said to me: "Hast ever had a nightmare?"

I said: "Often and one night I had a nightmare three times."

WESTMINSTER ROAD SALEROOM continued

FRIDAY NEXT. July 14
AT 1 o'clock
WESTMINSTER-RD.,
ELLESMERE PORT

YOUD AND LEWIS

Will sell by AUCTION as above
300 lots of valuable
Household Appointments.
On view Thursday and morning
of Sale
FURNITURE SALES
will be held every Friday, and all are invited
to include lots in these Sales. Sales conducted
on owner's premises. Valuations taken for
probate or transfer

● From July 7, 1925, Youd and Lewis had a regular advertisement, in which only the date in the top line was changed from one week to the next (with the result that there are always 300 lots of 'valuable household appointments' however many they really had!).

● Eventually he moved to two new sites. The 1934 Kelly's Directory of Cheshire records:

Youd Percy, auctnr. 56-58 Dock Street.
Youd Percy, furniture brkr. Cook St.

● By 1926 Percy – alone – had this advertisement in a regular "spot" on page two of the Pioneer, presumably with some financial subsidy from the monumental masons mentioned. What had happened to Lewis?

PERCY YOUD

Auction Rooms, 24 Westminster Road,
Ellesmere Port
Furniture Bought, Sold or Exchanged
OPEN DAILY 9 till 5
Sole agents for Williams and Sons
Sculptural and monumental masons, E. Port.
Monuments, tombs, headstones,
crosses or tablets in marble or granite.
Best worksmanship guaranteed.
Lowest possible prices. Deisgns and estimates given.
TERMS CASH.

Old Billy Mawsley [*sic*] said: "By the Hearty Mon, I only had it once and if I thought I was going to have it again I would commit suicide."

So someone asked what caused it, and I said the doctor told me it could be caused by lying with your arm underneath you – as I told the Doctor one Saturday night, I was afraid I would have the nightmare after he had cut a large cyst off my forehead just above the top of my nose. It was after 11 o'clock when he took it off. He promised to take it off in about two minutes – it had grown as large as a duck egg from Monday till Saturday, all through squeezing a blackhead out with my finger-nails. It was only like a pea on the Monday but grew very quick. I remember he put me in a big oak armchair that was screwed to the floor, then strapped my legs and my arms and chest and neck. I had to have my head leaned well back. I hardly felt him cut it out but he said he had to go to the skull bone to take the roots out. He made me shout! I think he was about 15 minutes; he used the knife first then a half moon shaped gouge like a wood chisel.

I said: "Take the straps off me," and he said: "Just a few moments. Do you feel faintish?"

I said: "Yes."

He gave me a drink of *sal volatile* so he said, then took the straps off. It was after 12 o'clock when he bandaged me up and then I had to walk about ¾ mile to my home. He put the cyst on a big soup plate on table near the chair. It was like a big goose egg.

I sometimes would not have a nightmare for over 12 months or more, then I might have it two or three times a week.

✳

● *A charming postcard of Phyllis and Leslie, dated 1918 and sent by Percy from Rock Ferry to his sister in Robin Hood Lane, Helsby. He says he has been off work "since week last Sunday, got hurt at work". He says he may be "over at the weekend with Phyllis". Had the separation from Sally already taken place?*

My old Dad used to say: "Perce, you have had more than your share of bad luck." I think the worst was once when I called at the Princes Hotel one Thursday afternoon to see if my nephew had brought my 12 bore gun back. I had lent it to him and he had said he would leave it at the Princes Hotel with my brother Alec, the licensee.

I asked my niece Gladys in the kitchen, and she said: "I don't know, my Dad is up in the sitting room up the stairs with Constable Charlie Twigg and his wife."

I went up and he asked: "What are you having?"

I said: "Nothing – it is half past three. I called to see if Eric had brought my gun yet."

He said: "No, but I will show you a grand firearm."

He went out and came back with a six chambered revolver, and handed it to Charlie Twigg saying: "What do you think of that, I gave a Canadian Captain £12 for it."

So Charlie pulled the breech open, then said: "This is loaded." He said: "Yes, but it won't go off." Then my silly brother pointed it at me and fired.

It hit me just above the right ear, went straight through my skull, came out on top of my head then went into the bedroom wall about two inches. [A little poetic licence here, we think; Ed].

I said: "You daft swine, get me to hospital, quick!"

Mrs. Twigg was screaming: "Charlie, put your handkerchief over his head!"

I was bleeding a lot from the two wounds, and my brother ran downstairs to phone the doctor, Police, and ambulance. Charlie Twigg told his wife to go and fetch a sheet from one of the bedrooms.

I said: "Give me brandy, whisky or rum."

● This postcard was sent to Sally c/o 11 Colliers Square, by her daughter Winifred on February 2, 1920, postmarked "Birkenmere". Winifred says: "Just a line to say we are quite well at present and hope you are the same. Will you send me a stamped address [sic] envelope to write to you. But do not mention this card when you write. Well you will wonder why I have not wrote but I thought it was your turn. Tell you news when I write."

The dark sepia card is the same as one sent to Gerald at Colliers Square on August 4, 1919 in what looks like Percy's writing. Only a cut-out fragment of this one, bearing tantalising scraps of a message hinting at the family situation, mentioning "your mother" and "being seen", remains.

He said "no," then threw his handkerchief in the fire, and held the sheet tightly over the two wounds. When my brother came in the room again, he said: "I have phoned the Police, ambulance, and doctor…" then started crying: "I would rather shoot myself than shoot my brother!"

I said: "You daft swine – you are not fit to have a catapult. Give me some brandy."

The Police said "No."

The doctor was over ½ hour before he arrived, just after the ambulance came.

Alec said: "Oh Doctor, I have shot my brother by accident! Let him stay here, don't send him to hospital."

After he had put dressings on my wounds the doctor said: "Take his coat off," and then he gave me an injection of morphia in my right elbow, saying: "He'll be asleep in ½ hour. Put him to bed, and he must not get up tomorrow. I will be here at 10 in the morning."

I said after the doctor went: "I shall not sleep this night, I am in too much pain. I feel as if the top of my head has gone off."

I asked the time. Charlie Twigg said 20 to 5 o'clock. My brother then went to phone my sister at Helsby and sister at Runcorn. I said to Charlie: "Try and get the bullet out of the wall."

I was still sitting in the big easy chair where I was when he shot me. Charlie got the bullet out and gave it to me. Just then my brother Alec came in and said: "I have phoned to Sis and Jane, my sisters."

I thought: "I am going to pass out soon." I had lent a chap £5 the day before and had no receipt or note to say I had lent it, so I thought I should tell them, but thought again that I would

● *Sally on a Helsby church outing to Blackpool.*

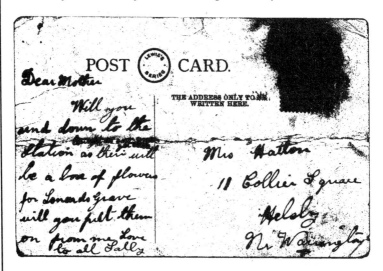

● *A sad postcard from Sally to her mother, sent on August 30, 1909: "Dear Mother, Will you send down to the station tonight as soon as you get this as their will be a box of flowers for Leonard's grave will you put them on from me, Love to all, Sally". Leonard had died in May 1909 and was buried at Helsby.*

not.

My Dad came up to see me at 6 o'clock; he was living at the Princes Hotel with my brother, and they went down for tea. He asked: "How do you feel, Perce?"

I said: "It feels as if the top of my head has gone and I am in awful pain."

He said: "I've seen thee in some queer doo's but never one like this. Will you have a drink?"

I said: "Yes Dad, fetch me a glass of beer, but don't tell any of them on the bar." And they could not see out of the kitchen as the door was shut and the stairs went to the bedrooms out of the hall. I drank the beer without taking the glass away from my mouth until I had drank the lot. I sat in same chair that night until 12.30am then went to bed in the room next to the sitting room. I never got a wink of sleep all night. I heard the clock strike every hour.

At 8 o'clock the manageress came to ask me how I felt and if I'd had a good sleep.

I said: "Never a wink," and she said: "Will you have a cup of tea, Uncle Percy?"

I said: "Yes, thank you, bring me two."

She said I had not to get up today.

A Detective named Baxter came next day, and said: "Now look here, Percy, if anyone asks you about being shot, say it was with an airgun."

I knew my brother had not a permit for the revolver and Detective Baxter was a pal of my brother's so it was hushed up. The ambulance was told by the Doctor it was not wanted, I was not to go to hospital.

I said: "I have been shot three times before at close range,

1907 - A POOR CHRISTMAS AT PRESCOT

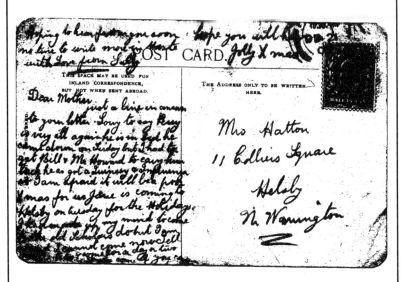

It wasn't only spectacular and bloody accidents that made Percy ill, in the era before antibiotics.

A pencil-written card from Sally to her mother, posted on December 21, 1907 says "Sorry to say Percy is very ill again he is in bed he came down on Friday but I had to get Bill and Mr Howard to carry him back he as got a Quinsey and Influenza so I am afraid it will be a poor Xmas for us.... Hope you have a jolly Xmas. Hope to hear from you soon, no time to write any more, in Haste with love from Sally."

● *Collins Family Medical Handbook says:*

Quinsy. A complication of severe tonsillitis resulting when infection causes pus to form within the tonsillar capsule, creating an abcess. Inflammation and accumulation of pus leads to severe pain and difficulty in swallowing...

A developed case will usually require the opening of the abcess and evacuation of pus, followed by antiseptic gargling. Immediate treatment should later be followed by removal of the tonsils since otherwise recurrence is common.

had the heel of my shoe blown off, on one shoot my pocket was blown away, and at another I was shot through my raincoat." At another shoot on Eastham Park one of the party put his gun on the grass next to me while we were having a snack and he had left the hammer cocked. He had gone few yards away, then coming towards where I was sitting he accidentally trod on the trigger. The gun went off, and I was nearly shot.

*

I saw a very funny thing one evening. I heard a rabbit squealing then saw a stoat doing somersaults in a circle and going on for a few minutes going smaller circles each circuit as he ran rings until he got to the rabbit, then seized the rabbit in the neck. I then shot the pair of them. I had been lying quiet under a bush. I have had as many as five rabbits with one barrel.

At Eastham Park one night just going dusk I shot a rabbit – I thought – but when I went to pick it up it was a hedgehog. Another time I saw a rabbit running in a small circle only about a yard wide. I thought it funny. I shot and killed it and when I went to pick it up found it was in a snare.

*

About a mile from Eastham along the banks of the Mersey near Price's Candle Works there was an old disused building and wall with 2ft 6in flat top. It ran along the shore to stop the tide. Near the building it was 4 foot above the ground, and one day when there was a high tide there was flocks of Redshanks all along this wall. I crept through some bushes and long grass

● *A bit of ice didn't put off those determined to go shooting! (Photo courtesy of Cheshire Record Office)*

● *Percy seems to have shot at everything that moved! This Wirral wildfowler at the turn of the last century has got a good bag of plump ducks, too. (Photo courtesy Cheshire Record Office)*

to the end of the wall and fired two barrels at these birds. There must have been 200. I killed and wounded many, put two more barrels in the flock as they came flying back over the wall to where many wounded birds were screaming. I collected 48 and counted 18 in the river which went away with the tide.

✳

I used to call at the Letters Hotel in Chester Street where I was friendly with the licensee John Lees, who introduced me to the late Captain Peel. Captain Peel told us about a pigeon shoot that was going to take place at Bangor-on-Dee in four weeks' time, and also a clay pigeon shoot to follow as a live pigeons shoot was illegal and had to be kept quiet. So John Lee entered me in the name of 'The Country Lad' and told me he would come over to Ellesmere Port with his car to take me to the shoot which was to be at six birds each, all guns shoot off same mark 25 yards from the Traps, 4 Traps, 60 yards Boundary. There were two bookmakers there, and a farmer named Tom Blake was favourite because he had been to shoot in the Grand Prix at Monte Carlo and had killed 31 pigeons without a miss, along with an American and an Italian. The same night he received an important telegram to return home and he did. Next day both the other two shooters missed their birds, so if Tom had not got the telegram he might have won the big International Prize.

I think there was only eight guns in the sweep; I was drawn No.1 so when I stepped on my mark John Lees shouted, "I'll lay 3 to 1 on the gun". I said to the trapper "pull!" so out came a Blue Rock Pigeon. I killed it with first barrel. In the second

PERCY BECOMES CONSERVATIVES 'A' TEAM SKIPPER

● *Percy's first mention in the Pioneer for bowling for the Conservative Club 'A' team is on Friday, May 1, 1925, when he scored the maximum 21 points against Conservative 'B' team member T. Knight. The 'A' Team won by 3 pts. Presumably he played for another club before this date as he was already known as a very skilled player. A fortnight later he is reported as having made "three of the best out of his game" and by May 22nd he is reported as being "the skipper" of the 'A' team (he lost by 12 points!).*

In the report reproduced below of a (lost) match against 'Recs' on May 29 the writer refers to his Helsby Hill Race success. The sports writing jargon of the day is as wonderfully cliché-ed as it is today!

...The visitors registered five winners, quite a meritorious performance on the Recs' green, as any trundler will tell you. Of these latter winners, real substantial scores fell to the lot of Fred Starkey who licked Bill Breeze 21–11, "Lenta" Catton, who stopped Sam Breedon at the 12 mark, and Perc. Youd, the visiting captain, who showed Tom Price that climbing Helsby Hill is not the only string on his sport instrument, he getting the homester in two minds at the 13 mark. J. Watson just scraped home by the odd one in 41, a vice versa remark applying to W. Simcox who near shaved J. Taylor.

round I killed with the first barrel again. Some had two barrels and some missed. I only shot my second barrel in the fifth round. I had wounded the bird but he might have gone over the 60 yard boundary if I had not fired my second barrel. I won the shoot by best average but shot and killed my sixth bird, but when the clay pigeon shoot commenced, the trapper tricked me by giving me a skimmer along the ground and when he did this for the second time I told him off. He had given all the other shooters what they call 'half mooners' so I told him off but shot at my other clay and did not try so I shot at six and missed them all.

We went back to Captain Peel's home, Abbeygates, after the shoot and it was lovely. I went over to visit him several times. His father, Major Hugh Peel, owned Bangor-on-Dee Racecourse and lived at Prennapiece Park about half a mile away. He had many accidents with his car and died at the age of 42. His only son was killed in the last few weeks of the War: he would have been very rich but got killed.

The first pigeon shoot at Bangor-on-Dee I went to was in 1931, the second was in 1932, and they came in a car to take me.

I said: "I am sorry, I have been sick all night and I've got cramp in the stomach."

They said: "Come with us, you need not shoot, we will get you some brandy."

They did, first in Chester, then at the Talbot Hotel in Wrexham, and then the Buck Hotel, Bangor-on-Dee. Captain Peel met us there at 1 o'clock then took us to Abbeygates for lunch. They told him I was not going to shoot through being ill. He told his butler: "Fetch a brace of guns out," and asked me which I would choose to shoot.

MOUNT MANISTY

● *Mount Manisty – rocks, rubble and rabbits surrounded by treacherous mud... (Photo by kind permission of the Cheshire Record Office)*

Mount Manisty lies between the Manchester Ship Canal and the River Mersey, just north west of Ellesmere Port.

It was made up out of the spoil removed whilst this section of the Ship Canal was being excavated, which was then dumped on the old Pool Hall Rocks. It is named after the engineer, presumably a Mr Manisty, who was in charge of this part of the project. Indeed it seems more logical to call it "Manisty's Mount" – as Percy does, though he spells it differently – than "Mount Manisty".

Percy and his son, Percy Jnr, used to go ferreting there for rabbits when they lived at Rock Ferry – a considerable distance away. Young Percy recalled in later life that he would cycle to Mount Manisty before school started. One morning he lost his ferret and his father sent him back after school to find it!

Now pock-marked with rabbit holes and overgrown with elder and brambles, Mount Manisty covers several acres and rises to 200 ft above the surrounding land at the western end.

Because of its proximity to Stanlow Oil Refinery, access is now limited for security reasons.

I said "Neither, I am not shooting."

He asked me how much did I think they were worth and I said "over a hundred." He told me they cost £250, they were by Purdy.

We called at Tom Blake's Farm for him, his son was the trapper and they begged me to shoot, saying: "You are drawn No.1 again," and I again won the shoot in 1932, killing all my birds.

I had four shooting rights about that time: one near Tarvin, Hockenall Hall, a very historical hall near the River Gowy. After ferreting there one Saturday we decided to stay for duck shooting at dusk for flighting time, there was four of us on the side of the River Gowy about 200 yards apart. All was quiet for quite a while. I was on the extreme right, I heard a shot, then a short while after heard a voice calling: "Percy, where are you?"

I shouted: "Here!" then one of the shooters, Charlie Price, a market gardener from Hoylake, came to me and said: "I have shot a big thing that came swimming up the river, looks like a badger. I shot him as soon as he got on the far side of the river bank."

I said: "It will be an otter," so we went about mile to cross over the Roman Bridge over the Gowy and found a dead otter.

Charlie said: "Throw it in the river," but I said: "No, we can sell him."

Charlie said: "If you can, we'll go halves."

We called at the Pied Bull, Chester, and Mrs. Shrieff said: "Give it to me for a neck fur."

I said: "He's worth 30/-," but she said "No." I took it to Birkenhead in Charlie's car and called to show it a shooting friend Denny who asked: "How much?"

I said 30/-. He paid me 30/- for it and sent it to be made into

● *Atmospheric photograph of Wirral wildfowler and his craft. (Photo courtesy of Cheshire Record Office)*

● *Shooters discussing tactics at low tide. (Photo courtesy of Cheshire Record Office)*

a neck fur. It was a lovely chocolate colour, and Mrs. Denny had it stolen at a whist drive.

*

Not long before this I had a very near escape from being drowned in mud banks between Manastys Mount [sic: Mount Manisty] and Stanlow Point. I was with a well known Sporting Chinaman, Charlie Chin, who was the interpreter for the Chinese in Liverpool. I left Charlie on the Canal Bank after rabbits, and said: "I will go across the mudbanks to see if I can find ducks in the big gutter about ½ mile in."

The Mersey tide was out when I left Charlie. I was about five yards from the big gutter, and came to stride across a small full gutter, but when I landed I went right up to my knees in mud and could not get out. I could not see the bank where I had left Charlie and started to shout for Charlie and not struggle. I got in an awful mess and must have been there nearly ½ an hour, then I noticed the tide was starting to come in. I was frightened and thought I must be in a quicksand near the place where a duckshooter named Hughes had been drowned many years before. As Charlie could not see me he came to follow my footmarks in the mud and had a great struggle to get me out. When we got to the bank between Manchester Ship Canal and the River Mersey I lay full length while he scraped the mud off me with a piece of wood then rubbed me with grass and I looked a real scarecrow. The tide was now coming in fast and I thought "another lucky escape".

*

Again, a few weeks later, I had arranged for Captain Peel

● *A party of more modern shooters sets out for some sport in a conventional boat. (Photograph by kind permission of Frodsham & District Local History Group)*

● *Shallow-draught boats, with or without tiny sails, could negotiate the gutters at low tide. (Photographs courtesy of Cheshire Record Office)*

and Councillor Walter Cross who was licensee of the Talbot Hotel, Wrexham, to come and have day's duck shooting on the River Mersey at Stanlow Point.

With Jack Hughes we went in his small rowing boat which was lying near his house in the stream called the River Gowy which runs under the Manchester Ship Canal by the Shell Oil Company Tanks and forms a large gutter running into the River Mersey. We sailed about 200 yards then he placed Captain Peel near the top of mudbank and about 200 yards away he placed Councillor Cross, then he took me about 200 yards further.

It was about tide time, and he was sailing back, when five ducks came right over me. I fired two barrels and hit two ducks which fell in the river gully between me and Councillor Cross. I called aloud for Jack Hughes to collect the two ducks which he did. Then he staked the boat and waited up the bank expecting a shot at duck, curlews, or geese and as the tide was getting higher I was wanting him to come and collect me. I thought of my lucky escape I had a short time before and now there was a strong fast tide nearly reaching me. I called loud for Jack Hughes to come to collect me but as the tide was now running fast he had a hard job to scull the boat against the tide, he just reached me in time to save me from being drowned.

We had a poor day's sport: they shot at several curlews but did not get any, so I gave them a duck each to take back with them.

Jack Hughes told us him and Arthur Dilworth had the record for a day's duck shooting, with a bag of 68 ducks with a 12 bore gun.

✳

● *The western tip of the massive Canal Deposit Dump, viewed from Rake Lane. (Photo AL).*

●*The bank of the Canal Deposit Dump in close-up, alongside the Hoolpool Gutter. (Photo AL).*

I must tell you a story about foxes taking Arthur Dilworth's turkeys. Both Jack Hughes and Arthur Dilworth lived next door to each other in the cottages at Stanlow Point between the River Mersey and the Manchester Ship Canal. Arthur traced the foxes to 200 yards past the old Fishermen's Ferry at Ince where thousands of tons of rock, sand, stone, and soil were tipped when the Canal was being made. It looks like a hill or small mountain, where lots of gorse bushes had grown and other plants. There was a large burrow of rabbits and many small rabbit holes. Arthur Dilworth invited me to go with him to shoot or blow the foxes up. He had traced the turkey to one large burrow where he had seen three or four fox cubs playing and he found many turkey feathers about one and half miles from his cottage. He asked me to meet him at Ince Ferry at 8 o'clock. He said he would come in his little motor boat.

I went to Ince on the 5.40am train and had shot eight rabbits on the Ince side of the Canal. I had shooting rights from the Gowy to Frodsham. At about 8.50am I heard Arthur's motor boat coming, I was then between the Rock Cutting and Ince Ferry. He came alongside the Ferry after being on night duty, he had left off at 6am and had washed and eaten his breakfast. He said: "I have brought lot of carbide, a gallon of paraffin oil, a bucket, also a bottle of petrol and a spade."

Operations were to start about 300 yards from the Ferry nearly atop the sloping bank. I had to fetch water about 100 yards; the bucket had a rope tied to the handle, and it was a very awkward job for me carrying the water. There were several small holes near the fox hole and many bolt holes. Arthur filled many bolt holes while I fetched the water. He had a small tin about the size of a salmon tin to get water out of my bucket.

LOADING SHELLS FOR KAISER BILL...

● Percy sent this embroidered postcard to his wife Sally from Quedgley in 1916. The X's may have been a private code indicating when he would be on leave, as well as kisses. Some of his remarks are intriguing:

"...many stopped away from Work here today thro report that Germans were going to blow up these Works today so I went to Work in the Works loading shells for Kaiser Bill hope he receives them..."

The wording seems strange for a soldier. Did Percy refer to where he was as "Works" simply from long habit of working in a factory – or had he been posted to some sort of munitions factory?

Quedgeley Nr Gloster
24th June 1916
Saturday Evening 6 o'clock

CARTE POSTALE / POSTCARD

Dear Sally (midsummer)
Just a few lines to you
hoping this finds you all
quite well at Home as it
leaves me A.I. many stopped away
from Work here to day thro report
that Germans were going to blow up
these Works to day so I went to
Work in the Work loading shells for
Kaiser Bill hope he receives them
best Love to all at Home from

Mrs Percy Youd X
Imperial Hotel
Prescot
Lancashire

give my best Respects to all
old Jake Jack Kaiser Bill Cack
Joe Pidge both Bill Davies. sticks
John Rainford Sephtons + all others
X X X X X X X X
Your Loving Husband Perce

He would throw a handful of carbide, throw it down the rabbit hole, throw a tin of water over it, then dig a sod to put over the hole. When he had filled them all up but one, I was then tying up my shoelace. He struck a match and threw the lighted match into a bolt hole. A terrific explosion went off. I must have been blown well up and dropped on all fours.

I said: "You daft thing, I have a good mind to shoot you!"

There was a large portion of bank blown away and I was very lucky I was standing on the edge of the crater. We did not find any dead foxes.

I was soon ready to go to the Duke of Wellington Hotel at Ince. When I got there Joe Ellis the licensee said: "Have you been shooting on the banks of the river?"

I said: "I've been blowing foxes up!"

He said there had been a big explosion either in the river or in the Canal, and the pub customers were saying they thought it was a ship's boiler!

Arthur Dilworth said he thought all the foxes there had been killed in the explosion as he never lost any more turkeys or saw any foxes afterwards.

∗

When I was in the Army in 1916 we went from Quedgley, Gloucester and arrived at Tidworth, Salisbury Plain at dusk. We were billeted at Multan Barracks, near the Oxford & Bucks. and 17th. & 21st. Lancers Canteen, who invited our Sergeants to their Canteen. I was the last of our Sergeants to leave and just before I got to our quarters I noticed a large black and white Persian cat. At first I thought it was a goat; it was very tame so I picked it up and took it to our quarters and no one

● *A young Percy with waxed moustaches and a rose in his button-hole, posing in a light-hearted mood for a professional photographer . He is pictured on a postcard sent by Sally from the Imperial Hotel to her mother in Helsby. She writes: "I hope you like the photo" and says she is "not keeping very well". Was that a polite way of hinting that she was pregnant again? The stamp has been scratched off, so there is no discernable post- mark to date the card, but it looks pre-WW1. Percy is his usual dapper self.*

was about so I went to see if I could find something to put it in. I found a large tea chest with a lid and put it in, tied it well with string, then got a post card out of my pocket, addressed it to my home, the Imperial Hotel, Prescot, then took it to Tidworth Railway Station which was about ½ mile away. No one had seen me pack it. At about 11.30pm I got to the station, had it weighed and paid the carriage – soon it was going on the 12 o'clock midnight mail train via Liverpool to Prescot.

Next morning there was a crowd searching for the Lancers' Mascot. There was many Regiments there and thousands searching for the Famous Mascot. I had not told anyone and I dare not as I was too upset.

The cat arrived at the Imperial Hotel but would not settle and became wild later. It lived on birds caught in my garden or rabbits that used to go in the large heaps of stone put in the field out of the rock cutting when they were making the railway to Liverpool. It was later shot by the farmer at a farm nearby.

✳

...Percy's story finishes here...

BIRKENHEAD

● *Left: Phyllis pictured in a group of 'senior girls' in a photo taken at Woodlands School, 1926, aged 12 years*

● *Right: a very thin Phyllis, aged about nine or ten, pictured while living at Hollybank Road*

Birkenhead, a Victorian boom town sometimes unfairly described as "Liverpool's ugly little sister", was once a seaside resort with bathing machines and donkeys.

In the period from 1800 to the late 1920s the population mushroomed in size from 100 to 147,000 people.

It notched up several notable "firsts" – the first public park (the model for New York's Central Park), the first tramway in Europe, and the first purpose-built library, workhouse and cemetery.

Birkenhead was developed firstly as a result of the establishment of a regular steam ferry service from Liverpool and secondly because of William Laird's initiative in setting up his shipbuilding and ship-repairing industry on its shores. He was responsible for the impressive Hamilton Square (named after his mother) and the formal pattern of roads emanating from it.

The town also boasted handsome stone-fronted villas and attractive Victorian semis and terraces. It was in a modest red-brick bay-fronted house of this type that Percy Youd lodged with three of his children.

THE STORY OF PERCY YOUD'S DAUGHTER

**Percy Youd's wife Sally left him in 1918. Their marriage dete-
riorated irrevocably after she is believed to have forgotten to
apply to renew the licence for the Imperial Hotel in Prescot
while her husband was away. Percy never forgave her. They
had had eight children, three of whom had died in infancy.
This story is by their daughter, Phyllis, Ken Bazley's mother:**

Only the scratching of pens and occasional cough broke the
silence of the classroom. Suddenly the door opened and a child
came to the teacher's desk with a note from the Headmistress.
Looking at the children in front of her, the teacher called to a
thin child with long straggly hair: "Put your books away, the
Headmistress wants to see you."

The child, who was about ten years old, looked up nervously, put away her books and walked out of the classroom along
the corridor to the Headmistress's room. There behind a large
oak desk sat the Head, but not looking stern as usual, her neat
grey hair scraped away from her face. Behind her gold-rimmed
glasses her eyes twinkled as she smiled at the pathetic little girl
– so pale, with a pale mauve dress under her gym slip, and
lace-up boots. She understood only too well that the child
should have worn a white blouse under her gym slip, but
knowing the pupil's background she didn't scold her. Instead
she smiled at the girl, her smile softening the face that was usually so forbidding, and with a firm but gentle voice she said:
"Get your coat and go out of school to the main gates. Your
mother is waiting to take you and your brother out for the day."

That child was me.

● *Charing Cross, Birkenhead. (Postcard from AL's collection).*

● *The ferry, Birkenhead, in the 1920s with Liverpoool in the background. (Postcard from AL's collection).*

I could hardly believe what I heard, but knowing that the Head never lied and was a strict disciplinarian, I stammered a nervous 'thank you' and passed through the door. Hurrying along the corridor to the cloakroom I took my coat off the hook and ran to the steel stairs, down three flights and out into the large yard which led to the main gates.

There standing waiting patiently was my mother, a tall neatly-dressed woman in black with a large-brimmed hat. Her clothes were clean and tidy but obviously working class. A smile lit up her face when she saw me, her youngest daughter. My mother was a good-looking woman but the radiant smile made her look really beautiful. Standing beside her was a boy of about twelve, also very thin and shabbily dressed – my brother, Leslie. Mother and I looked at each other rather shyly, as this was the only occasion of the year when she came to take us to Liverpool to see the Christmas grotto and to get what was needed in the way of clothes. Although we saw her during the long summer holidays, this was an outing we never forgot and looked forward to eagerly.

So hand-in-hand Leslie and I walked beside our mother to the Underground station and the train that would take us all to Liverpool. Everywhere in the city the streets were beautifully decorated for Christmas and all the people seemed happy as they did their shopping. We went from shop to shop, our eyes bulging with excitement. We went to Lewis's, a large department store, to see the grotto which was so beautiful that we could hardly speak. And of course at the exit of the grotto was Father Christmas in his bright red costume, his magnificent white beard and whiskers wobbling as he laughed heartily, asking each child what he or she would like for Christmas.

● *Queen's Memorial and Town Hall, Birkenhead, c1909. (Postcard from AL's collection).*

● *Substantial Victorian semi-detached houses in Park Road South, Birkenhead, c1911. (Postcard from AL's collection).*

Then came the magic moment when he dipped in his sack for a blue parcel for Leslie and a pink one for me. Clutching our treasured presents we rejoined our mother, who stood smiling at us as we came out.

Another treat was in store for us as she took us up in a lift to the Red Rose Restaurant right at the top of the store. Here again as we ate our meal of chips, sausage and egg, followed by Christmas pudding, Mother's face shone with pleasure as she watched us tucking into the food. When we had finished eating, we went out of the store and crossed the road to Blacklers, where Mother bought new boots, underwear, a gym-slip, blouses, shirts and trousers for us. Laden with parcels, it was time for Leslie and me to go back to Birkenhead, so we returned to the Underground, all very happy but tired.

Parting was always sad, but all our exciting purchases made it easier for us children to say 'good-bye' than for our poor mother. She made her way back to the station to catch the train to the cottage in Helsby where she lodged with our eldest brother, Gerald. She worked very hard every day going to different houses to do washing, ironing and cleaning for the "upper classes" as they were called. Also, if anyone in the area died, she would be asked to lay them out, for which she received the princely sum of five shillings. She was loved and very highly thought-of everywhere. One very large house where she worked used to give their servants a party every year and she was always invited to it – but was also asked to keep her eyes open as some of the servants invited friends and the lady of the house trusted her to keep the place in order – because when it was party night the family were always away. So she was in a position of trust as the silver was very valuable.

● *Left: Phyllis's elder sister Winifred Youd, dressed in her finery for a formal portrait.*

● *Colliers Square, centre, pictured from Helsby Hill in the early 1900s. Phyllis now lives in the house in the foreground on the right. The barn has been demolished.*

She had a long walk of about two miles to get to the party but she didn't seem to mind it and, of course, she knew every corner of the house and grounds, which were in a beautiful setting with the hills of Frodsham in the background.

The village where she lived was also a pretty place and the house where she lived nestled under Helsby Hill. All the people knew each other and were always ready to help one another in times of need. Colliers Square, where she lodged with the Cartwright family, was a happy little group of working class people.

Mr and Mrs Cartwright had one son, Cyril, and three daughters, May, Alice and Emily, so it was a tight squeeze with very little space for everyone and the landing had to improvise as a bedroom. But they were a happy family who also loved and felt sorry for Mother and Gerald, so they put up with things to help her until she could save enough to rent a little cottage of her own. This was her one dream, to reunite her divided family: our eldest sister Winifred was in service as maid to a rich family in Sefton Park in Liverpool, so she didn't see a lot of Winnie, and our father, Percy, Leslie and me, all lodged in Birkenhead.

It was all so sad after the hard life Mother had known, especially as she'd had her own servants when we were all living as a family in Prescot at the Imperial Hotel. There had been eight children altogether, including the three little boys who died – Leonard, Sidney and Cyril. They had been brought back to Helsby to be buried. Sad to say our parents' domestic life had not been happy; eventually Mother left my father, and with Gerald and me (I was only two at the time), she came back to Colliers Square, initially living with her mother Lizzie Hatton at

● *The block in Hollybank Road where the Youds lodged. (Photo by AL).*

● *An atmospheric view of Argyle Street South, Birkenhead, complete with tram (right). Hollybank Road is not far away, to the left. (Postcard from AL's collection).*

No. 11. She never had a penny off my father after they split up: she was much too independent.

Like Mother, "Granny Hatton" (as she was known) was also loved by everyone – people always knew that she would help them in confinements, illness or deaths. When I was small I remember hearing that she used to "lay people out". I was very innocent and thought it meant she hit people over the head and knocked them senseless! This dear little old lady with her black old-fashioned bonnet and cape, and boots, could often be seen trudging along with her bag of comforts from one end of the village to the other.

One day when I was only about three or four, I was playing happily with a doll which a friend of my mother had given to me – it was all dressed in clothes the lady had knitted and it was my greatest treasure. Suddenly, my father came along, picked me up and took me to the station to get the train for the Wirral, where he lived. As we were going down Station Lane the lady who had given her the doll saw them and went to tell her mother that she had seen my father with me and that I was crying and clutching my doll. So at least Mother knew where I was. She eventually claimed me back, but one day my dad came again with a taxi and took me off to Birkenhead.

I can remember that Dad lived at Rock Ferry for a short time when I was little. Then we had to leave – I was too young to understand why – and I can recall walking round Birkenhead with him and the others, looking for somewhere to stay. A policeman directed us to *Mrs Duncan's house in Hollybank Road and she took us in.

We lodged with Mrs Duncan for years. She was a very eccen-

* Not her real name

● *The first alleyway (above) at the side of the block in Hollybank Road leading to the second alleyway (below) at the back of the houses, pictured in December 2002. (Photos by AL).*

tric lady who would often gaze into a crystal ball and said she could tell the future. She would dance round wearing beads, with feathers in her hair. She made her own hats with lots of flowers and feathers. She made me look in her crystal ball one night, and I imagined all sorts, as you can imagine.

She liked Leslie but she took a dislike to me and made my life a misery. We went to Woodlands School and after I came home in the late afternoon and was sitting on the horsehair sofa by the step up to the back door, with my hair all straggly because no-one was looking after it, she would grab me by the hair and throw me out. I never told my father.

As we grew older Dad often took us to the market on a Saturday night and bought us sweets, then he would leave us to go back on our own to Hollybank Road. We were nervous of the dark and always held hands. We had to go up two dark alleyways to the back gate past the outside lavatory. When we got in Mrs Duncan would go out to meet Dad at the Argyle Theatre. It was the country's leading music hall – the London Palladium of its day. George Formby had his first professional performance there and you could see people like Harry Lauder, Stan Laurel, Charlie Chaplin, and Flanagan and Allen.

Once she left us alone, Leslie and I would lock all the doors because we were so nervous. We were always hungry because Mrs Duncan didn't give us proper meals, so on a Saturday nights we would steal some sugar and Quaker Oats, mix them together and eat the mixture out of our hands – because we daren't use dishes.

She never cooked meals for us. I recall one day when she made a rice pudding specially for our dad: we would have loved some but we never got any. Why didn't he stick up for

● Above and right: Sally Hatton (later Youd) as a child, pictured at school in Helsby in the late 1880s (she was born in 1882). (Photograph reproduced by courtesy of Herbert Fletcher)

● Left: Granny Hatton outside her house in Colliers Square, with Phyllis's cousin Lance Hollingsworth (who emigrated later to Canada or Australia).

us? I suppose he just assumed that we'd had our food before he got in – but we hadn't.

The one meal I could look forward to each week was when I went out to tea on Sundays to the Broster family, whose house in Hazel Road backed on to Mrs Duncan's across the alleyway. Mr Broster was a policeman and I was friendly with his daughters Eva and Eleanor.

Leslie, Percy and I all used to sleep in one room. Dad had the big bedroom at the front of the house.

There was a bathroom upstairs, but we two children weren't allowed to use it; we had to wash in the scullery and use the lavatory down the yard. When it was dark we would light a candle and, having gone hand-in-hand down the garden path, one would hold the candle while the other went in.

We were not usually allowed to come into the house through the front door. One moonlit night when a little girl called Nellie Clark had been murdered locally my brother and I thought we saw a man with a knife in the back alley. We were too scared to go near so we ran round to the front door in a panic and hammered on the door. Mrs Duncan let us in. She was so strange: do you know – all her windows were nailed down!

She used to send me to fetch paraffin for the lamps. One day, I was skipping along and fell over and broke the bottle, cutting my hand. She wasn't bothered about my hand but she was mad about the broken bottle.

I got into trouble once because I was knocked down by a taxi. We were playing a game where I was dashing across the road to touch the railings by the school, and this taxi came along and ran into me. I don't think I was very hurt. Dad made me stay in the house every night for a week after school as a

● *Phyllis (drummer boy, kneeling on the right) in the Helsby Girls' Bible Class production of "Aladdin".*

● *The cottage in Bates Lane rented by Sally Youd, shown decorated in red, white and blue bunting (made by Winifred and Phyllis) for George V's jubilee. Their efforts won the first prize of 10 shillings.*

punishment.

Dad was an auctioneer at Ellesmere Port when we lived at Hollybank Road. He had a wooden building near the Conservative Club and I was so proud because his name was on a sign there. It read: "P. Youd, Auctioneer." I remember he also had an advert on the safety curtain at the cinema, and I thought that was great.

He would often take me to the saleroom on Saturday mornings to see what had been entered in the latest auction and if there were any pianos there, he'd try them all out. I remember being fascinated one time by some big Chinese masks.

He used to keep some of the more unusual things that he'd got through the business and put them in the front room at Hollybank Road. I remember there was a stag's head on the floor that I was looking at and I fell on the antlers! I had to have my bottom stitched up by the doctor, lying across a chair. Also in the room was grandfather clock that he'd won in the Hill Race.

My father also kept his collection of strange objects that he'd amassed at the Imperial, including the calf with two heads, stuffed birds and so on. The calf was kept with many of the other things in a greenhouse in Mrs Duncan's garden, and we let slip at school one day that it was there. All the children came round to see it!

Dad spent a good deal of time at the Conservative Club and would bring us back treats of chocolate. He was very good in that we never once heard him run our mother down. In fact, he never used to speak about her, except I remember one day he said to me: "Do you want a bike?" I got really excited, thinking he might have one at the auction, and said: "Yes!" "Then go

● *Leslie Youd played cornet in the Helsby Silver Band. Fellow musicians in this group are: back row, left to right, Herbert Fletcher, Gordon Fowles, Tommy Hopley, Hubert Ellams; front row, Leslie Youd, Ron Walker, ?. Below, the band pictured playing for Helsby Flower Show and fete in 1936 (names unknown).*

and tell your mother you want a bike," he replied. I never had a new bicycle of my own until my brothers bought me one for my 21st birthday.

At Birkenhead we had a lot to do with Lock Ah Tam and his family. Tam was very generous and he held a party every year for the Chinese children. One year we went with the Tams to a party in Chinatown in Liverpool. They handed us chopsticks but Mrs Tam – who was English – spoke to one of the cooks in Chinese and he brought us some spoons. I also remember going to the seaside with them. The girls, Doris and Cecilia, were very attractive, with long black hair down below their waists. They were riding on the donkeys when one of them got into some barbed wire and her hand was cut very badly.

I was suffering from toothache on the night that Lock Ah Tam killed his family. Dad came home early from the party to see how I was getting on. I sometimes think that if he'd stayed, he might have been there when it happened. After the court case, when I was 11 years old, I went with him to Birkenhead Market when he was gathering names for the petition against the hanging of Lock Ah Tam.

I remember that Dad had a Shetland pony that we used to walk up to Tranmere. I think he had several horses over the years because there were some stables at the saleroom.

He also had "Bonzo" a full-size white wooden rocking horse that had been used for teaching soldiers to ride. He eventually gave it to Ellesmere Port Council and they put it in the park [see p154]. I would have loved to have had it!

As we were growing up our father allowed us to go to Helsby for the school holidays, which was a much looked for-ward-to treat every year. The good kind people of Colliers

● *A very faded snapshot of that exciting Ship Canal picnic. Phyllis is pictured at the front, posed lying down and drinking from a botttle. With her (left to right) are (back) Bill Davies, her brother Leslie, Hector (later sister Winifred's husband), Arthur Davies and (front) Alice Cartwright, Emily Cartwright and Winifred.*

● *Phyllis (right) camping with the Girl Guides, after her return to Helsby – having benefited from the "kitchen medicine".*

Square were there always ready to help out, so I was squeezed into the Cartwright home and other neighbours used to let Percy and Leslie sleep at their house, until Percy started work in Liverpool in the Liver Buildings.

One summer holiday when I was twelve and Leslie nearly fourteen, the Sunday School trip came up and Dad said we could go on the trip or go to Helsby. Of course we chose Helsby. What we didn't know was that Mother had saved up and rented a little cottage not far from Colliers Square and had been busy furnishing it. So on this day off we went to Helsby – as we thought for a day out – but our brother Percy had been in touch with Mother and it was all arranged. Once Mother got us there she kept us and young Percy quit his job in Liverpool to come and live with us, leaving our father on his own. So the family were reunited at last – for Winnie had moved to be in service at Helsby – and Dad was on his own at Birkenhead.

The little cottage in Bates Lane was now home to Mother, Gerald, Percy, Leslie and me. Every day she would go out to the big houses to wash and clean for them.

On that fateful day when Leslie and I took the train from Birkenhead to Helsby, I tried to dress up a bit so I put a white blouse on top of my gym-slip to look different. We arrived at Helsby from the station, and walked up to Bates Lane where Mother was waiting on the doorstep in her large white apron to welcome us. We'd no idea that we wouldn't be going back to Birkenhead.

Mother had arranged with all her friends – the Cartwrights and the Davies – to take us on a picnic to the Manchester Ship Canal. In advance they had collected bacon bones and string to catch crabs. The group took food and a large black kettle and

● Above: Phyllis with her splendid first new bicycle – a present from her brothers.
● Left: Brother Leslie in band uniform standing outside the Bates Lane cottage, with its cobbles on the right.

● Phyllis married Edwin Bazley in 1938. This part of their wedding photo, taken at 18 Brittania Gardens, Helsby, shows the Youd family. Back row: Sally, Percy Jnr, Leslie, Gerald; front row: Edwin Bazley, Phyllis, Joan (Les's wife), Ivy Booth (Phyllis's niece).

off they went across fields and ditches which meant crossing planks down the marshes. It was very exciting for us all. When we arrived on the banks of the Ship Canal all the children collected sticks and bits of wood to light a fire while the grown-ups set out the food. While the kettle was boiling we children took the string and bones to catch crabs, just for the fun of it. There was a small bay where we sat to drop our lines to see who could catch the biggest crab. It was so exciting, and what a different life from the one Leslie and I had been used to in the urban surroundings of Birkenhead!

The country air and the good food which our mother cooked for us began to give us a bit of colour, for I was practically a wreck by that time. I suffered from nightmares, dreaming that Mrs Duncan was in the bedroom, dancing round the bed wearing strings of beads – which she used to do when we lived with her. I was so frightened.

But as I gradually got used to the peace of Helsby, plus the good diet and fresh air, I settled down and became much better, although I have been anaemic and pale for the rest of my life as a result of being half-starved at Mrs Duncan's hands. Mother fed me on what she called "kitchen medicine" – good nourishing food. Once on the advice of the doctor she gave me raw liver sandwiches and the nurse came to administer iron injections, which helped to build me up.

After I left school I got a job at the cable factory in Helsby – "the B.I.", as we called it. Once, I had tonsillitis very badly and was sent to the BICC rest home at Whitford near Holywell to convalesce. A lot of men from the works at Prescot were there too. My mother came to visit me one day and the men were really pleased to see her. They remembered her with great

PERCY YOUD'S FAREWELL

News of Percy Youd's death made front page news in the Ellesmere Port Pioneer of Thursday, October 3rd, 1963:

HE 'BUGLED' M.P.

Death of Mr. P. Youd

MR. Percy Youd of 1 Grace-road, who invariably greeted Mr. Selwyn Lloyd with a bugle call whenever the M.P. visited the Conservative Club, died in Clatterbridge Hospital on Saturday at the age of 84.

Mr. Lloyd had visited Mr. Youd in hospital last Thursday.

For many years, Mr. Youd was a familiar figure on the bowling green, winning many prizes. He was also a wellknown athlete in his younger days, gaining awards for running and long-distance walks.

One occasion he won the Helsby Hill Race in 8 minutes 16½ seconds, a record time.

In the children's play area in Whitby Park is a wooden horse which he presented to the Council.

affection from her time at the Imperial, and said they recalled me being born.

My father called on me once or twice after I got married but he would never come inside the house. We didn't have much contact when I was grown up.

I thought his parents were rather weird. I remember my grandfather was a little old sunken man and my grandmother seemed to spend her time knitting socks for us grandchildren.

Dad was a very, very popular man. He always had plenty of friends. He was very generous, and if someone admired something of his, he would be quite likely to give it to them.

He frequently took shooting parties out and when I was little if he took me with him to Carlett Park he would sit me down under a tree and tell me: "Sit there and don't move!"

He was very keen on bowls and often went to the Isle of Man to play. He won lots of cups. After he died we couldn't find a single one when we went to clear out the house. He must have given them all away.

He liked nuts and had a habit of keeping a handful in his pocket which he would crack with his teeth. Perhaps, with hindsight, he shouldn't have! I've been told he got septicaemia after pulling out an aching tooth with pliers and eventually died as a result.

Dad was a very self-centred person. He enjoyed being the centre of attention and in spite of his generosity he sometimes didn't give much consideration to other people. I suppose as far as the family was concerned, he thought he was the bread-winner and that was all that mattered.

I remember being told that when we were at Birkenhead he bought a train set for my brother Leslie. Then it disappeared

XF 586487

CERTIFIED COPY of an ENTRY OF DEATH

Issued at a fee of one shilling in pursuance of and for the purposes of the First Schedule to the INDUSTRIAL ASSURANCE AND FRIENDLY SOCIETIES ACT, 1948.

Registration District ....Wirral.

1963 DEATH in the Sub-district of ......Clatterbridge........in the.......County of Chester

Columns:—	1	2	3	4	5	6	7	8	9
No.	When and where died	Name and surname	Sex	Age	Occupation	Cause of death	Signature, description, and residence of informant	When registered	Signature of registrar
218	Twenty eighth September 1963 Clatterbridge Hospital Bebington	George Thomas Percy Youd	male	84 years	of 1 Grace Road Ellesmere Port. a Retired Watchman	1a Bronchopneumonia b Hypoplastic anaemia Certified by John E.Davies M.B.	P.Youd Son 1 Freshmeadow Lane Helsby-via-Warrington	Thirtieth September 1963	M.C. [illegible] Registrar

I HEREBY CERTIFY, that the above is a true copy of an entry of death in a Register Book in my custody.

Witness my hand this............Fourth...........day of..........October..........19 65 ....[signature] Registrar.

Person to whom issued:
Name and surname (in full)......Phyllis Bagley
Address.........Underhill, Old Chester Road, Helsby-via-Warrington

Relationship to deceased : child, adopted child, stepchild, grandchild   (Delete those inapplicable.)

CAUTION:—Any person who (1) falsifies any of the particulars on this certificate, or (2) uses a falsified certificate as true, knowing it to be false, is liable to prosecution.

Percy's death certificate. Did pulling out a tooth with rusty pliers hasten his demise?

one day and Leslie saw it in the window of a nearby pawn shop. Dad hadn't said a thing to him about it.

Although he claimed he hadn't had much schooling, he was bright – for his own ends – and quick at figures. He was a pretty sharp businessman and he used to buy and sell land. He had shooting rights all over the place.

He had quite a bit of money at one time but he lost it – I don't know how. By the time he died he'd got through all his money. He certainly didn't leave me any!

Dad's funeral in 1963 was a low-key affair and after he was cremated my brother Percy scattered his ashes off Freshmeadow Lane, Helsby – which seemed appropriate as he had always enjoyed shooting on the marshes nearby. In those days there were only houses down one side, where my brother lived, and the rest was just fields.

My mother died three years before Dad. She was buried in Helsby cemetery where the twins and Leonard had been laid to rest so many years earlier.

Phyllis Bazley

XE 305241

CERTIFIED COPY of an ENTRY OF DEATH

Issued at a fee of one shilling in pursuance of the INDUSTRIAL ASSURANCE AND and for the purposes of the First Schedule to the FRIENDLY SOCIETIES ACT, 1948.

1960 DEATH in the Sub-district of .... in the COUNTY OF CHESTER

Registration District ....

No.	When and where died	Name and surname	Sex	Age	Occupation	Cause of death	Signature, description, and residence of informant	When registered	Signature of registrar
172/15	Twenty third May 1960 Britannia Factory Kirkby	Sarah Jane Youd	Female	78 years	wife of George Thomas Youd Percy Youd a general labourer	1a Carcinoma coln. 1b Pernicious anaemia. Twenty certified by T.B. Brown MB	P. Youd Son Factory Lane Kirkby	Twenty fourth May 1960	W. Davies Registrar

I HEREBY CERTIFY that the above is a true copy of an entry of death in a Register Book in my custody.

Witness my hand this .... 24 .... day of .... May .... 1960 .... W. Davies .... Registrar.

Person to whom issued :
Name and surname (in full) .... Phyllis Bagley ....
Address .... Old Factory Plas Kirkby ....

Relationship to deceased : child, adopted child, step-child, grandchild. (Delete those inapplicable)

CAUTION:—Any person who (1) falsifies any of the particulars on this certificate, or (2) uses a falsified certificate as true, knowing it to be false, is liable to prosecution.

Sally's death certificate. She is still described as the wife of Percy Youd – "a general labourer".

158

BIBLIOGRAPHY AND SOURCES

The Internet is a wonderful tool for research. However, where very specific website addresses have been given, there is unfortunately no guarantee that they will remain unchanged. If you are interested in further research, try them and see what happens!

● *Frodsham and Helsby, The Archive Photographs Series*, compiled by Frodsham and District Local History Group, published 1995 by The Chalford Publishing Company, Stroud, ISBN 0 7524 0161 0.
● *Frodsham – The History of a Cheshire Town"*, edited by Frank A Latham, published by Local Historians 1987; ISBN 0 901993 06 9 / 0 901993 07 7.
● *Frodsham in old picture postcards*, Joseph Barker, European Library; ISBN 90 288 2334 4
● Frodsham & District Local History Group photographic archives
● *Memories of Marsh Lane*, Pat Ellams, Frodsham & District Local History Group, Autumn 1990 Newsletter, Issue 10.
● *The Licensees of the Public Houses in Vale Royal*, A J MacGregor.
● *Kelly's Directories* for 1882, 1895, 1914, 1934, 1939; *Morris and Co's Directory* 1874.
● *'Open the door and let us in!" by Roy Clinging,* published in The Living Tradition Issue 25, also www.folkmusic.net/royclinging/clinro_arts. htm
● *Traditions similar to Hoodening* by Ben Jones
http:/ourworld.compuserve.com/homepages/bj1/hood/bjhoodsi.htm
● *The Old Ways: Hallows* by Doug and Sandy Kopf
www.cyberwitch.com/wychwood/Temple/hallows.htm
● *The Horse's Head Play - The Lymm* Version www.thelwallmorris.org.uk
● *Soulcaking Play performed at Lymm, 1930* (ditto)
● *Frodsham Soul Caking Play (as recited and sung by Bob Rodgers)*, Frodsham and District Local History Group
● The Earl of Stamford Morris, *Halton Souling Play*
www.dl.ac.uk/TCSC/CompEng/EOS/Souling
● *The Helsby Story, 'Modern Industrial Age 1-2', W.I. Yearbook* extract
www.angelfire.com/pa/helsbynews/archhist2.html
● *History of Automatic Telephony,* web.ukonline.co.uk/freshwater/histauto.htm
● *A History of Cable Making at Helsby Factory,* L G Banbury, June 1980
● *1901 Census information,* www.census.pro.gov.uk
● *Naxos Nostaligia, George Formby*
wen02.hnh.com/scripts/Artists_gallery/other_artists.asp?artist_name=Formby
● *Manchester 2002/3, Papillon Graphics' Virtual Encyclopaedia of Greater Manchester,* www.manchester2002-uk.com/history/victorian/Victorian4.html
● *The Manchester Ship Canal, a brief history*, MSCCo

www.shipcanal.co.uk/Pages/history-pages
- *The Manchester Ship Canal* by W T Perkins, c1909
www.fls.org.jm/users/worldeng/manship
- *Prescot Town local community website,* www.prescot-town.co.uk
- *Knowsley Local History, Prescot* http://history.knowsley.gov.uk
- Prescot Museum local history resources
- Greenall Whitley archives
- *Ellesmere Port – The making of an Industrial Borough* by Peter J Aspinall and Daphne M Hudson; edited and with contributions by Richard Lawton, published 1982 by the Borough of Ellesmere Port, Neston, South Wirral; ISBN 0 5076 660 7.
- Numerous editions of *The Ellesmere Port Pioneer*, 1920-1963
- *The Illustrated Portrait of Wirral*, Kennth Burnley, Robert Hale, London 1981/87
- *Ellesmere Port Town Pack, Frodsham Town Pack, Helsby Town Pack,* Cheshire Libraries and Museums
- *Murders that made headlines*, Ken Whitmore, The News, 23/04/1973
- The Ordnance Survey for extracts from 1910 maps
- The Queen's Royal Lancers www.qrl.com
- *The Tidworth Journal* www.tidworth-village.co.uk
- *Cheshire Country Houses* by de Figueiredo and Treuherz (Phillimore 1988).
- *Album of Photographs of Wildfowling on the Dee* which originally belonged to Mr L N Brookes of Gayton Cottage, Heswall and is now at the County Record Office, Chester.
- Personal papers and photographs of Mrs Phyllis Bazley

INDEX

INDEX

British Insulated Callenders Cables
(BICC) 32, 56
    Rest Home 153
    Sports Day 54
British Insulated Wire Company iv, 30, 56
    Sports facilities 64
Bromlow, Joe 85
Broster, Eleanor 145
Broster, Eva 145
Broster, Mr and Mrs 145
Brown, Old Father 27
Burial Certificates 88
Burkhill, Fred 39

C

Carlett Park, Eastham 73, 155
Cartwright, Alice 139, 150
Cartwright, Cyril 139
Cartwright, Emily 139, 150
Cartwright, May 139
Cartwright, Mr and Mrs 139, 151
Catapult 11
Charnock, Jack 61
Chatto Heath 61
Cheshire hills iv
Cheshire Sheaf, The 22
Chester 1, 15, 63, 67
    Auction Mart Sale 67
    Commercial Hotel 37
    Pied Bull Hotel 67, 121
    Town Hall 37
Chester Castle 15, 66, 71
Chester Chronicle 13
Chin, Charlie 123
Chiu, Mr 68, 69
Chiu, Mrs 70
Clark, Nellie 145
Clay pigeon shoot 10, 117
Coal Strike 59

Connahs Quay 57
Cook, Colonel 63
Crabs 151
Crosland, E 28
Crosland, Mr Joe 59
Cross, Councillor Walter 125
Cupola furnace 52

D

Dace 41
Davies Family 151
Davies, Arthur 150
Davies, W 83, 150
Dean, J 83
Death certificate 156, 158
Delamere Forest 3, 47
Denny, Daniel Patrick 62
Denny, Mr 69, 121
Denny, Mrs 123
Dilworth, Arthur 125, 129
Dogs, Champion Show 97
Domino matches 1
Dooley, Private 63
Duck shooting 125
Duncan, Mrs 141, 153
Dutton, Jack 103

E

Earnshaw, Mr 31
Eastham 44
Eastham Park 115
Eden, Sir Anthony 87
Ellams, Hubert 148
Ellesmere Port iv, vi, 51, 67, 85
    Conservative Club vi, 67, 71, 83, 100, 118, 147
    Dock Street 106
    Grace Road x, xiii
    Marsh Farm Cottage Pontoon x
    Princes Hotel 83, 103, 109

INDEX

INDEX

INDEX

Léonie Press local books include:

MEMORIES OF A CHESHIRE CHILDHOOD – MEMORIAL EDITION
Lenna Bickerton (ISBN 1 901253 13 9) £4.99

"WE'LL GATHER LILACS..."
Lenna Bickerton (ISBN 1 901253 21 X) £5.99

DIESEL TAFF
From 'The Barracks' to Tripoli
Austin Hughes (ISBN 1 901253 14 7) £8.99

A NUN'S GRAVE
A novel set in the Vale Royal of England
Alan K Leicester (ISBN 1 901253 08 2) £7.99

NELLIE'S STORY
A Life of Service
Elizabeth Ellen Osborne (ISBN 1 901253 15 5) £5.99

THE WAY WE WERE
Omnibus edition incorporating Over My Shoulder and Another's War
Les Cooper (ISBN 1 901253 07 4) £7.99

A HOUSE WITH SPIRIT
A Dedication to Marbury Hall
Jackie Hamlett and Christine Hamlett (ISBN 1 901253 19 8) £8.99

WOOLLYBACK   *(A novel set in Winsford)*
Alan Fleet (ISBN 1 901253 18 X) £8.99

A WHIFF OF FRESH AIR (plus CD)
A collection of humorous Cheshire monologues
Margaret Dignum (ISBN 1 901253 20 1) £9.99

MID-CHESHIRE MEMORIES – VOLUME 1
The Horseman and his Family; The Apprentice Mechanic's Tale;
The Apprentice Fitter's Tale; The Fireman's Tale of the End of Steam
E E Osborne, G Mellor P Buckley and B Fisher
(ISBN 1 901253 28 7) £8.99

**From Léonie Press, 13 Vale Rd, Hartford, Northwich,
Cheshire CW8 1PL.   Website: www.leoniepress.com**